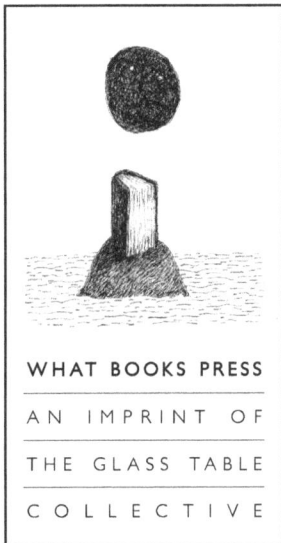

WHAT BOOKS PRESS

AN IMPRINT OF

THE GLASS TABLE

COLLECTIVE

LOS ANGELES

ALSO BY CHUCK ROSENTHAL

Loop's Progress

Experiments With Life and Deaf

Loop's End

Elena of the Stars

Avatar Angel: The Last Novel of Jack Kerouac

Never Let Me Go
MEMOIR

My Mistress, Humanity

The Heart of Mars

*Are We Not There Yet? Travels in
Nepal, North India, and Bhutan*
MAGIC JOURNALISM

Coyote O'Donohughe's History of Texas

WEST OF EDEN: A LIFE IN 21ST CENTURY LOS ANGELES

CHUCK ROSENTHAL

WHAT
BOOKS
PRESS

LOS ANGELES

The author wishes to gratefully acknowledge the the editors of the magazines in which the following
chapters have appeared: "Are You Awake My Darling" in 88, "Collapsing with the Stars" as
"Colapso estelar: vida literaria al pie del letero de Hollywood (Alicia Partnoy, translator) in *Luvina*,
and "Collapsing With the Stars: Literary Life Under the Hollywood Sign" in *Luvina On-Line*; "My
Chicken Obsidian" in *The Offending Adam*; "East of Hollywood" in *Shimmyhoots*; "What Is Magic
Journalism?" in *Intellectual Refuge*.

Publisher's Cataloging-In-Publication Data

Rosenthal, Chuck, 1951-

  West of Eden : a life in 21st century Los Angeles / Chuck Rosenthal.

  p. ; cm.

  ISBN-13: 978-0-9845782-8-3

  ISBN-10: 0-9845782-8-5

  1. Los Angeles (Calif.)--Social life and customs--21st century. 2. City and town life--California--
Los Angeles--21st century. 3. Celebrities--California--Los Angeles. 4. Rosenthal, Chuck, 1951- 5.
Rosenthal, Chuck, 1951---Family. 6. College teachers--California--Los Angeles--21st century. I.
Title.

F869.L85 R67 2011

979.494/054   2011914265

What Books Press
10401 Venice Boulevard, no. 437
Los Angeles, California 90034

WHATBOOKSPRESS.COM

Cover art: Gronk, *untitled*, 2012
Book design by Ashlee Goodwin, Fleuron Press.

WEST OF EDEN: A LIFE IN 21ST CENTURY LOS ANGELES

For Gail

CONTENTS

The Afterward   11

My Chicken, Obsidian   13

Immortality   26

Ask the Dust   35

At the University of La-La Holy   45

I, Jesus: The Life of Jesus in Los Angeles   48

Gabriela   51

Sea Mingo   56

Collapsing with the Stars   59

A Good Man Is Hard to Find   65

East of Hollywood   70

The Ten of Writer   86

Trader Joe's, a Parable, a Prophesy   90

At the University of La-La Holy   94

Health and Education   98

The Life of Jesus in Los Angeles: The Early Years   105

Two Little Terrorists from La Boca   111

At the University of La-La Holy: The Traffic of Unicorns   114

Hostage: A Hollywood Parable   119

At the University of La-La Holy: The Perfect Stain   125

24 Hour Grill   138

At the University of La-La Holy: "A" for Lack of Effort   142

The Life of Jesus in Los Angeles: Jesus Cures the Blind Boy   144

The Book of Cleavage   146

The Great Escape: Do Not Go Gentle   148

A Literary Agent in Los Angeles? The Birth of Magic Journalism   154

The Goddess Dies, Nightly   160

The Life of Jesus in Los Angeles: Jesus Raises the Dead   162

The Xmas Party   164

The Life of Jesus in Los Angeles: Jesus Among the Hamburger Sellers   169

Sometimes Si! Sometimes No!   171

Masters of the Poetry Universe   177

The Prague of War   181

Jesus Is Transfigured   187

For Jimmy Skaggs   189

Are We Not There Yet? or Daze of Future Past   191

Preface: What Is Magic Journalism?   194

THE AFTERWARD

(BECAUSE LIKE MOST INTRODUCTIONS
IT WAS WRITTEN LAST AND PLACED HERE)

THE FOLLOWING is an essay of Magic Journalism, neither fiction nor non-fiction, neither fact nor fict. Though I hope it's often metaphorical and occasionally poetic, neither is it poetry, though briefly I contemplated calling it creative non-poetry, a term that I believed I'd thought up on my own, but found I'd been pre-empted by poet Richard McAnn. So, as to not bias your reading, or worse, tell you how to read, I've placed the Preface, "What Is Magic Journalism?" at the end. Of course, the book is in your hands. You're welcome to turn to it at any time.

MY CHICKEN, OBSIDIAN

BECAUSE EVERYTHING DEPENDED on a red wheelbarrow next to a black chicken in the rain. Or did it depend on Sting? Let's start with the chicken. My lover, the poet Diosa, had a friend named Mervyn Delamore, a gay Filipino-American-Jewish-Indian chief who, like Diosa, was infatuated with Dolly Parton. And chickens. Long phone conversations consisting of Dolly Parton lyrics. That coat of many colors my mama made for me. Mervyn said he knew Dolly. She cooked him country breakfasts (eggs, eggs from his own chickens, and bacon) and woke him up with cocaine instead of coffee. Mervyn knew everybody. He'd slept with Richard Gere and Mick Jagger and Andy Warhol. Mervyn was always pulling that "she'd really prefer me over you if I wasn't gay" thing on me. How do you explain to a woman that that bugs you? So maybe it wasn't about chickens. Chickens were just so many flightless birds.

Until a chicken walked into my house on the winter solstice. Then we found out who liked chickens and who didn't. I was standing at my front door watching a plumber and his assistant drain the septic tank when a big black chicken with green highlights walked into my kitchen.

"That your chicken?" said the plumber's assistant.

"No," I said.

"Is now," said the plumber.

"Nice chicken," the assistant said. He rubbed his stomach with his hand and licked his lips.

She was a nice chicken. I named her Obsidian.

Diosa was in Malibu with her mother, Jin-Jin, visiting from Laguna Woods. I called her cell. "A chicken came to our house," I said.

"Is it a nice chicken?" said Diosa.

"It's a pretty nice chicken."

"I knew he was going to get a chicken," said Jin-Jin. Beings from other spheres spoke to Jin-Jin and told her the future, which she kept to herself until it happened. When something already happened Jin-Jin always knew ahead of time. The past always confirmed the future. In other parts of the world that's called schizophrenia, but in Los Angeles it's called religion.

"Pick up some scratch at the Feed Bin," I said.

"We should call Mervyn and ask him what to do," said Diosa.

"I'm not asking Mervyn what to do," I said.

"Because you're homophobic," said Diosa.

"Tell Shark I'm not sleeping with the chicken," said Jin-Jin.

That's where it stood with the chicken. Now Sting. My old friend Serum Pallapatti, a Dravidian-looking Indian born in Fresno had somehow become a wealthy Hindu masseuse to the stars, one of them Sting. How do these things happen?

I met Serum a long, long time ago up in San Francisco because I was fucking his roommate. She wasn't Serum's girlfriend, she was Diego Maradona's girlfriend, but he wasn't around much. Nonetheless, he always left lots of good coke. We made love sitting on her leaky waterbed, face-to-face, while Serum wrapped his twenty foot python around us. Serum said that's how Hindus did it. You think Tantric sex is hard; it's not on a waterbed with a twenty foot python wrapped around you. This is the difference between San Francisco and Los Angeles and if I have to explain that it'll ruin it.

Ten years later I was running my dogs in Red Rock Canyon and there was Serum walking toward me down the road. It was hot. We were only a mile from where the killer bees were supposed to invade from Calabasas.

"I thought you'd be dead by now," he said.

"I thought you'd be dead by now," I said.

No, we'd been reborn in Los Angeles as responsible family men.

So one day he burned down his ice cream parlor near the Top o' Topanga and used the insurance money to build a yurt. He'd decided to make a living giving bad advice. He figured there were two things people didn't want, good advice and free advice. He went downtown and made love to a judge. That's what he said, though you can't believe Serum about that kind of thing. Regardless, he convinced her to send him Robert Downey Jr. who had just been arrested again for possession of cocaine. What could it hurt? Robert Downey Jr. was hopeless.

"What do you do for him?" I said.

"I hold his hand till he falls asleep," Serum said.

Anyway, he convinced Downey that he'd feel a lot better if he unloaded all his worldly possessions. Downey was no fool and experimented by giving Serum a bunch of money and his wife's BMW SUV. His wife divorced him. I don't know what helped but something in that made him feel better. He found a new wife, got off coke. Serum still holds his hand, but the pay is good. On the other hand, it didn't work for Mel Gibson.

Diosa and I were at Serum's eating curried goat when Mel called.

"Serum," said the voice on the machine. "It's Mel. Help me. Serum, help me."

"That's Mel Gibson," said Diosa.

Serum shrugged the shrug of ten thousand years of deep spiritual Hindu indifference.

"You're not going to pick up?" I said.

"Everybody responds to him," said Serum. "Nobody tells him 'Fuck you.'" He opened a cigar box and started rolling a joint. "He's a train wreck," Serum said.

Was Serum a Hindu? Of course not. Did he have chickens? Yes, lots of them. Did this strategy help Mel Gibson? No. That was back during the Jesus and Apocalypto phase. Gibson was a coke addict. He was coked up on the night of his anti-Semitic outrage outside Moonshadows. When my friends visit from back east I ask them, "What do you want to do? Take the kids to Disneyland?" No. Moonshadows. So maybe Serum helped Mel. He's more famous than ever. I saw him last night on Leno pushing his latest movie, new lover, new baby, chattering like a maniac, feet bouncing and repeatedly rubbing his finger under his nose.

"Isn't he Catholic?" I said to Diosa.

"Like the Pope," she said. "One of the ones with fourteen kids."

Chickens, Catholics, Hindus, chickens. I see Mel up at Serum's but he doesn't say hello.

All of the homeless where I live in downtown Topanga Canyon were once famous. Eli discovered plate tectonics. Ted taught Stephen King how to write. Daryl wrote all the songs for Little Feat. Stephanie made nature films in the 70's with Jacque Cousteau and taught Washoe sign language. Rafer gave Cameron the idea for Avatar. Maya ran the Latin Grammies for Michael Green. They bought homes, lost their jobs. If you own a home then there's no hope for you. Famous people moved to the canyon, bought homes and fell into the abyss.

I ran into the once famous poet, Poet Dan, down at the General Store where Diosa sent me to buy a frozen pizza and a bottle of Smirnoff, a pack of Parliament Lights, you know, a break from our bad habits.

"Want to hear a love poem for fifty cents?" said Poet Dan. His red and gray mustache hair grew down to his chin.

I gave him a dollar. "I'm against love," I said.

"How's that chicken of yours?"

"She's not my chicken. She's a chicken of the world."

"Chicken of the universe," Poet Dan said. He wrote that down on his scrubby pad. "Heard you want to get rid of her."

Well everybody in that canyon knew everything about everybody else or thought they did. I liked the chicken but for the fact that she did sleep with Jin-Jin when she visited and she liked to peck my daughter, Jesus, on the head and she pooped inside the house. Nonetheless, she made the cutest sounds when she sat on your lap.

"I like the chicken," I said.

"Diosa says it's going to be her or the chicken," said Poet Dan.

"How would you know?" I asked him.

"Us poets know what other poets are feeling."

Let me tell you, I know more about poets than you'd ever want to know. Shake a tree in Los Angeles and a poet falls out. I suppose I could have talked to Diosa about the chicken but it would have destroyed the implicit texture of our relationship.

"Talk to your neighbors," Poet Dan said.

"What neighbors?"

"I'm a poet, not a messenger," said Poet Dan.

I got home and gave Diosa her cigarettes.

"I'm leaving you," she said.

"I know already," I said. "For who?"

"I'm thinking about it."

So I picked up my chicken Obsidian and went next door where my neighbor Clea Duvall and her girlfriend, Radio, lived. Technically, Clea slept in her 1975 Pontiac Firebird Trans-Am because she didn't want to jinx the fame thing. That house had rickety stairs, no interior wiring, just extension cords. You could see through the walls. It was such a wreck it was only worth a million dollars. The last guy who lived there, Ken Waverly, was the inventor of the skim board. You haven't heard of him because he bought that house and dropped off the end of the world. He was Genevieve Bujold's nephew and kept ferrets. Once he came back from Cabo and invited us to a big fish barbecue where Genevieve Bujold and her sister sat on my lap. They were still pretty cute and it pissed Diosa off.

"*Excuse moi!*" said Diosa.

"You are excused," said Genevieve Bujold.

Clea and Radio came to the door. They were both tiny. Radio was dark and Goth. She had a rock band and Jesus, who played sitar, went over and jammed with them sometimes. Clea was blonde at the time though you wouldn't know it because they both tucked their hair under black longshoreman's caps pulled down over their foreheads. Jeans, boots, black leather jackets. Radio had a '75 Trans-Am, too, a big firebird painted on the hood, Georgia plates, of course. She worked on the cars out front while listening to Southern rock.

"Heard Diosa's leaving you," Clea said.

"It's an old story," I said to her. "Sometimes she's gone for minutes at a time, right in front of my face."

Those two didn't smile much but that got a smirk out of Clea, that same smirk you've seen on the screen.

"But it's not our chicken," Radio said.

"She could visit," I said.

"We don't want a chicken," said Clea.

"We're still getting the ferret smell out of here," Radio said.

Clea petted Obsidian on the head, who clucked. "That's a nice sound," she said.

"But we don't want her," said Radio.

"You don't have to live in your car," I said to Clea.

"I'm on a roll. I don't want to blow it," she said to me.

"Look at me," said Radio. "Doomed. Look at you."

"I never fell from fame," I said to her. "I rose to obscurity."

"Nobody told us until it was almost too late," Clea said to me. "I'm glad I never really moved in."

"Close enough," said Radio. "She'll end up on television. Just wait."

This is a town thick in the mystical. But clairvoyant as that interlude turned out, I still had my chicken. We tried locking her out but she flew from deck to deck and followed the cats through open windows.

"I thought chickens couldn't fly," said Diosa.

"She's eating all the cat food," I said.

"Why not give her to Serum?"

"He won't take her from me. It's a guy thing," I said. "You give her to him."

"He knows it's your chicken," Diosa said.

"If everybody knows everything around here then why does everybody know that Obsidian is my chicken but nobody knows whose chicken she was before that?"

So I finally called Mervyn.

"Emmy Lou Harris just made me breakfast," Mervyn said.

"I think she's a Christian, Mervyn."

"So's Dolly," said Mervyn. "So what? She opened for the casino. Then Mick came by and gave me a watch for my birthday."

"Richard Gere gave you a watch for your birthday last month."

"Mick's always late," he said.

"I thought the casino was dead in the water," I said to him. The last I'd heard, Coppola and the other wine makers put a thumb on Mervyn's casino. The quiche crowd didn't want low rent gamblers mucking up Sonoma County.

"These No-Cal liberals are Indian hating hypocrites. We had to build them a new sheriff's department and a new jail and produce Coppola's next movie," Mervyn said. "But the metal buildings are up, slots are in, we broke ground last week."

"Mafia money?"

"Wealthy Italians from Las Vegas, Señor Tiburon. Don't throw that M-word around, it could get you in trouble."

"Will you take my chicken, Mervyn?"

"I don't have hens," said Mervyn, "only roosters."

"That's baloney," I said.

"Anyway, Leonardo keeps the chickens at his place." Leonardo was his new boyfriend.

"Can I give her to Leonardo?"

"I don't let him accept chickens from other men," Mervyn said.

"You chicken lovers are the hypocrites," I said to Mervyn. "Diosa's going to leave me if I don't get rid of the chicken."

"It's about time," said Mervyn. "Tell her she can manage the stage at the casino."

Anyway, you might think I'm friends with Serum, but I'm not. Neither of us is that friendly. He's Diosa's friend. They get stoned and drink coffee up at the Circle. Ignoring famous movie stars and charging them for bad advice or no advice had made Serum a wealthy man. He was a notorious womanizer and being rich helped a lot. Diosa, on the other hand, was notoriously beautiful, an ifriti, a huri. I don't want to get into it, but men fell in love with her on sight, powerful men, celebrities. Gary Busey went down at the Malibu Pharmacy, Martin Sheen at the Cross Creek Coffee Bean and Tea Leaf, Brad Pitt in the Colony CVS. It's why Angelina Jolie left him. Diosa said she had a very low voice. George Clooney swooned out at Topanga Days. Nick Nolte on the bumper cars at the Malibu Fair (back east we called them dodgems).

Nick Nolte really pissed me off. He already had two women half his age following him carrying big net bags full of stuffed animals. Turns out he's great at carnival games. He got in his bumper car followed by fifteen middle aged women all trying to hit him at once. He turned his car and hit Diosa head-on, fell out his car with his tongue out, stopped the ride. Drunk. Didn't keep him from jumping up and following us to the basketball shoot. You know the routine, two tiny iron baskets eleven feet up. Me and Nick.

It was usually my element. I could hit baskets and give stuffed tigers and bears away to a standing mob of children until the carnie shut me down. But not that night. I missed. Nolte hit. "Ha!" he said and gave Diosa a stuffed panda. I missed and he hit again. "Ha! Ha!" he said and gave Diosa another panda. Again. "Ha! Ha! Ha!" Another panda until I pulled Diosa away, dragging her out of the Fair and into the parking lot with Nolte and his toy bearers hot on our heels. At our car door Diosa gave him back the pandas and he wept.

It was pretty quiet on the ride home.

"Nick Nolte crushed you at basketball," said Diosa.

I'd been humiliated by a drunk celebrity. So she could leave me in a moment. Why not?

"I'd have to listen to them," she said. "They have nothing to say."

So anyway, all those people who didn't know who really owned my chicken Obsidian figured Diosa was sleeping with Serum.

"So what do you talk about with him?" I said.

"Sting."

Yes, Sting. After a day of listening to New Age music through Bose headphones in Serum's mountaintop yurt, Sting felt so much rage for having spent the day downed out and listening to mediocre, New Age music that he discovered an even deeper rage, a deep rage deeper than his self had ever admitted—well, if not his self, then at least his persona—a rage which brought him to the realization that he needed to write his autobiography. Serum was good at what he did, whatever that was.

Now Serum was on my answering machine.

"Hey, Shark," Serum said to the answering machine because, like him, I never answered the phone, "Sting's going to write his autobiography. I know you're there. He already got a million for it from MacMillan and he hasn't written a thing."

My daughter, Jesus, picked up. "Dude," she said.

"Dude," said Serum.

"No, you Dude," said Jesus.

"What did he have to say about it?" I asked her later.

"He said Ben Stiller wants to see one of your funny books."

"He can see them at the bookstore. Everybody just wants free books," I said.

"Dude," Jesus said.

"Dude?"

"We use it facetiously, Father Dude," Jesus said.

"Sting didn't get a million dollars because he's a good writer," I said to her.

"Get some distance, Father Dude," she said. "Engage space, the final frontier."

"Do you mean ironic distance?" I said.

"Your education has alienated you," said Jesus.

"Alienation is a kind of distance," I said to my daughter.

"Serum needs me to baby sit for Robert."

"Robert's kids?"

"No, Robert. I do it all the time. He's staying at Sting's this week."

But then Diosa came home from the Target with dozens of platform sandals, even three pairs for Jesus and a gray pocket T-shirt for me. Gray is my favorite color. Diosa always bought something for me so I'd be implicated in the purchase. She believed that the moment just before buying something, when a woman held her credit card in front of the salesperson, was the only time a woman held any power in Los Angeles. So it was ontological.

"They were on sale," Diosa said.

> She dropped the black bags on the faint red
> tile   kitchen floor   I stood pale in
> front of the bags of shoes   A white shoebox fell
> out and fell   open   Out the window, fog came
> over the distant cliff as if from China and Diosa
> fingers like doves, bent slowly to the sandals lifting
> one by a heel strap, stepping from one shoe
> into another, and then   again   Her hair fell
> upon her shoulders, her ankles shifted, her skirt
> floated   kissed her knees

Okay, she wasn't wearing a skirt. In my mind she was wearing a skirt. But even in her black Capri pants her legs drove me crazy. Apparently they drove a lot of people crazy.

"They were practically giving these away," said Diosa. And you couldn't save a cent on them if you didn't spend anything.

Diosa looked me in the eyes, her jewel blue eyes glowing with what she didn't have to say about spending money: my sweet little horse. $2,500 a year on board. $600 a year on horseshoes, if you wanted to talk about shoes. Vet bills. Swimming pools. Movie stars. And two Xmases ago she'd bought me a motorcycle. Regardless that it was half my money, she'd bought it. Not a fat ride either, but a crotch rocket, the kind all the young organ donors rode up and down the canyon. She called it my Kawasaki Viagra.

She stepped into my arms. She wore her hair just over her shoulders, blonde and blue in the front and weaving into auburn, black, and red on her back and shoulders; high cheekbones, a strong nose. Though medium height, she could look down on anyone, so when she looked up, when she chose to look up at me the thrill was beyond description; her body so soft, so remarkably soft that I found the idea of someone living within it unimaginable, and yet there she was, fully willed and fully self-imagined. We went to her office, chased her brown dog off the futon. Shut the double shutter doors. She took off her clothes and my clothes and she put me in her. "Now," she said, "about that chicken."

So it was Diosa or the chicken. Without a plan, pulling at last straws, I got my chicken Obsidian out of the house. I took her to Sting's. Sting's place was the last one on the street of the Colony, a Moroccan castle with a retractable roof. In the front entrance, his swimming pool was surrounded by a jungle. Just indoors, the hot tub, filled with imported sulfur water, was so deep you could stand in it. He had a TV screen bigger than my house, a kitchen the size of Manhattan. Outside, through the giant living room window, a pod of dolphins leapt and frolicked near his private beach.

"That's amazing," I said to Jesus.

"They're always here. He rents them," Jesus said.

I'd brought Jesus and Serum's two daughters, Ashley and Celine, and my chicken Obsidian. Robert sat on the couch holding the remote and giggling at the TV where the movie *Chaplin* was playing. "Hee-hee," said Robert. He pointed at the screen. "That's me! That's me!"

"He loves to see himself in movies," Jesus said to me.

"Think he'd want a chicken?" I said.

"I doubt it."

"Do you think Sting would want a chicken?"

"Oh Father," said Jesus.

Robert had his son there, Indio. "Indie, Indie, come here, look, that's me!" said Robert.

"Oh Father," said Indie, looking at Jesus. He held a soccer ball, dropped it, and he and Jesus headed into Sting's huge kitchen to play soccer.

Ashley and Celine began opening and closing Sting's roof. I put my chicken on the floor.

"This is my favorite movie!" said Robert to somebody.

For my part, I've always been amazed how such a funny guy like Robert could make such a tedious movie about such a funny guy as Chaplin.

Sting's roof opened. Sting's roof closed. The soccer ball hit Robert in the back of the head. Robert ignored it. "Come watch this movie!" he said. "I'm in it!"

My chicken Obsidian tried to jump on Robert's lap, but he elbowed her off. "Next *Iron Man*!" said Robert Downey Jr.

In the kitchen, the soccer ball rebounded from the huge pots hanging from the ceiling and brought them clanging to the floor. The roof opened. The roof closed. Celine emerged wet and naked from Sting's hot tub. My chicken pooped on the Moroccan rug. "Look, that's me!" yelled Robert Downey Jr. And then Sting came in the door.

Everyone ignored him. He ignored everything. He went to the kitchen, got himself a bag of dried Japanese kelp, came back into the living room and stood next to Robert.

"That's me," Robert whispered to him, pointing at the TV screen.

"What's Robert Altman's chicken doing here," Sting said.

"Isn't he dead?" I said to him.

Sting looked at me quizzically, I think noticing me for the first time.

Robert jumped up. He began to dance around with his hands clasped over his head like Snoopy in the old Charlie Brown cartoon. "Junior!" yelled Robert Downey Jr. "Junior! Junior! Junior!"

At home, Diosa was packing. She was moving to Sonoma, changing careers, abandoning poetry to run Mervyn's Indian casino.

"You'll be back," I said.

"Not if that chicken's here."

"There are no shoes in Sonoma," I said. "Everyone goes barefoot. They don't wear makeup in northern California. There are wild animals and there's nothing to drink or eat but wine and pie."

"Pie?"

"The Indians gather at the Santa Rosa Carrow's at midnight. They eat nothing but pie. You'll be an alien."

"I'll be a fashion revolutionary," said Diosa.

"Give me one last chance," I said.

I got Bobby Altman Jr. on the phone.

"Bobby," I said on the phone, "I think I have your chicken."

"My chicken is dead," said Bobby Altman Jr. "I no longer own a chicken."

"You don't own her because she's at my house."

"I saw her die," said Bobby Altman Jr.

"On the solstice?"

"What's the solstice?"

"Around Christmas."

"A coyote chased her over my fence. I saw it."

"She came to my house," I said. "She's black with green highlights."

"I don't think that's my chicken," said Bobby Altman Jr.

"I'm bringing her over," I said.

"Oh please don't do that," said Bobby Altman Jr.

"Where are you going with our chicken?" Jesus said to me as I gathered up Obsidian from the cat food bowls.

"Our chicken? What have you ever done for this chicken?"

"A page on Face Book?"

"She's Bobby Altman Jr.'s chicken."

"Don't go there, Father. There are Scientologists over there."

Needless to say, this was only making too much sense.

Bobby Altman Jr. lived just on the other side of Clea and Radio. He bought the house from an iron sculptor named Norm Grochowski who sold the place because his wife, Ciri, left him. She moved to Arcata and he followed her. If you live in Los Angeles then you know the progression: Venice Beach, Topanga Canyon, Arcata. Folks from Malibu move to Laurel Canyon and then Oregon. I don't know why Ciri left Norm but I was beginning to suspect it had something to do with my chicken Obsidian.

When I got there, Jesus was right, the place was crawling with positivity. A naked blonde stood breast feeding a two year old in the kitchen doorway. She had black concentric circles drawn around her breasts. "Bulls eye," she said to me.

"Have you seen Bobby?" I asked her.

"You're the chicken guy, huh," she said.

"No he's the chicken guy," I said.

"You're holding the chicken," she said. "Is that your motorcycle down the street?"

"The yellow one," I said.

"Why didn't you ride it here?"

"Because it's only twenty yards away and I'm holding a chicken?"

"You're in denial. You're afraid," the woman said. "Face your fear."

"If I were afraid," I said to her, "then not riding my motorcycle would be facing my fear and riding it would be denying my fear."

"Do you want to make love to me?" she said.

"I'm just going to leave this chicken here," I said.

"Don't leave that chicken here!" yelled Bobby Altman Jr. He came from the living room.

To be honest, until the day before, I didn't know there was a Bobby Altman Jr., likely because of the huge mistake he made in buying this house.

"Take a look at her."

He covered his eyes. "I can't look," he said. "My chicken is dead."

Suddenly Scientologists came pouring into the room, through the doors and windows; it seemed they were walking through walls.

"Bobby Altman Jr. is in denial about this chicken!" I yelled at them.

"I'm not a Scientologist!" yelled Bobby Altman Jr.

But just then a pleasant, middle-aged red head, Evelyn Altman Jr., it turns out, came in from the yard. "Pepper!" she said. "You found Pepper!"

My chicken Obsidian jumped into her arms. Evelyn wept. Bobby Altman Jr. wept. Hell, I wept. Anyway, there was a red wheel barrow in the kitchen and that's where she put my ex-chicken Obsidian.

I don't think Sting ever wrote his autobiography. He just took the money and ran. Mervyn's casino construction hit another snag. Zoning. Environmental waste hazards. Down here you can put a casino in your front yard, but up there you'd need a space ship. Bobby Altman Jr. moved. Diosa stayed, for now. I don't know where my chicken Obsidian is. Everything's the same. Nothing has changed. Everything in Los Angeles is illusion. It's not a Hollywood thing, it's a Hindu thing.

IMMORTALITY

I don't want to do anything forever.
Anthony Flew

IN MY FIRST fifteen years in Topanga Canyon, Memorial Day was a bacchanalia, the culmination of three days of Canyon celebration called Topanga Days. In the morning there was a parade of a hundred homemade floats. Bands played on the backs of trucks. People dressed as animals. They rode unicycles and walked on stilts. War veterans marched carrying the flag while women danced around them baring their breasts.

But the best part was the water. Folks armed themselves with squirt guns and water rifles, or extended hoses from their homes and shot at the floats. And the floats shot back. Fire trucks loaded with kids moved in the parade line. The kids pointed out their parents and had them blasted with the water cannon. Yet with the right timing you might slip under the angle of fire and nail your son or daughter, or better, your neighbor's kid who you had to be nice to 364 days and twenty two hours a year and put a column of water right between his eyes.

The nudist colony, Elysium Fields, had a float where the members covered themselves with only mud. You can imagine how that ended up.

Some years we lined the street, other years we turned my truck into a float, one year robots, another *Hair*; we duct taped a CD player to the roof and played theme music, we filled garbage cans full of water so we could replenish our pump rifles with a simple dip and pull. Our friends Mingo and Gabriela and their daughters Eva and Anahi, Serum with Ashley and Celine, me and Diosa and Jesus; we filled the back of the truck. The adults took turns driving. Commandanté Mingo organized us so we always had half of us loading and half firing while Serum and I dropped off either side of the truck bed and assassinated acquaintances up close. For two hours on one Monday morning out of the year we got to go stone sober crazy.

Then it ended. A coalition of Prius drivers, the Topanga Elementary Charter School PTA, $500 baby carriage owners and farmers' market types bound together to outlaw water on Memorial Day. That's right. Liberals. They outlawed water.

In Topanga Canyon it's now illegal to carry a squirt gun on Memorial Day. Because if you carry a squirt gun you might squirt somebody. Worse, it's a bad example for children who might observe adults having a good time. You can carry a .44 Magnum in the Topanga Days Parade, but not a squirt gun. Armed State Troopers line the parade route. In the first year of the prohibition I stood in the back of our float with a plastic bottle of water. I raised it in the air. "Water!" I yelled. "Water!" I was arrested. Confined. Prevented from attending Topanga Days.

I vowed never to attend again, but you know what happens when you make a vow like that. Diosa agreed with me until Memorial Day morning.

"Come on, Shark," she said, "let's go."

"I have a hangover," I said.

"Everybody has a hangover. We'll drink beer at the carnival."

"Beer's a liquid," I said. "It's probably outlawed."

"Only in the parade," Diosa said.

"It's not a carnival anymore, it's a shopping mall." This was truth from a madman. In the water fight days you could drive your float right into the festival for free and park it on the baseball field. Now the baseball field was lined with merchandise booths, the floats banned from entering, and it cost $20 a head to get in.

"I'll go with Serum," Diosa said.

"Fine."

"I'll let him give me a Hindu massage in public."

"You're not scaring me," I said.

"Everyone will think the worst."

"Everyone already thinks the worst."

"Do it for me, Shark," said Diosa. "I'll wear a skirt."

That's how easy I am.

Parking for Topanga Days is hell. Cars stretch down the canyon for miles. The road is clogged with State cops and tow trucks ready to ticket and tow any vehicle parked within a hair's width of the pavement. You walk a mile or so through all that, then up the hill to the Community Center, pay your twenty bucks. The theme this year, on a banner at the entrance: "Immortal Topanga."

Inside the place is mobbed with people pretending to be Topangans, men in odd hats, hippie chicks with cleavage. Booths sell scarves, crystals, beer can sculptures, scarves, crystals, ceramics, scarves, crystals, jewelry, henna tattoos. There's food, too. It used to be homemade on site, now it's restaurant outlets. Between the booths the aisles are thick with humanity, body to body. Once, everybody brought their dogs and horses, but that's not allowed anymore. Now they bring children, though it's not the best place for them. There's a little row of kiddie booths behind the Community Center building—those everybody wins games like Fish Pond—a clown paints faces. I don't like kids or clowns so I stay clear.

Inside the Community Center building there's a stage with picnic tables where the local kids belly dance, perform karate, or play in pre-teen rock bands. Jesus' first band, Tinkle, played here. In back there's a stage for acid bands and out front there's a big stage at the bottom of a hill where the featured bands play, mostly Seventies rock or reggae; people dance in front on the dirt, chicks on shrooms, guys barefoot and shirtless, they dance and dance all day; you can walk up to them and have a dance if you want. There's not much shade but for a big oak tree behind the stage. That's where you want to be, but that's where everybody wants to be.

I grabbed a couple beers and Diosa and I walked among the hundred merchandise booths outside the Community Center building. Shopping, shopping, shopping. Diosa can shop in a closet; it's in her genes. But you run into people you know; it's still a small community and most of us are here, including all the water fight anarchists who vowed never to come again. I wander with my beer, wander back, find Diosa at the next booth over. Get us more beer. It's better than the mall. We're outside. There's beer. The hills of Topanga, filled with sage and manzanita and oak trees, roll and roll, appearing infinite if not immortal; the sky is California blue. Tomorrow everyone will be gone and I'll ride my horse and run my dog down some abandoned trail.

We've passed through the hundred booths and stand at the top of the hill above the stage. The shroomers are dancing. Hippies age fifteen to sixty-five are swaying. We're partying like it's 1973. Beyond the stage, on the baseball field below, five hundred more booths of scarves and crystals stretched out like the bazaar in old Mosul.

"Think there are any shoes in there?" I said.

Diosa's eyes glistened.

"Okay," I said. "Let's do it."

We circled the stage and headed into the booths. Hours, days, weeks; what is time? What is money? Or as a rug merchant in Old Delhi said to me, "You give me your money and I give you a rug. I give someone else the money. They give it again to yet another person. It goes on forever and the money disappears, but you, for the time being, you have a rug." Time, time, time, as Vegeta said on *Dragon Ball Z*. Time to send me to the next dimension.

We were making our way back toward the big oak tree when we ran into Serum.

He was wearing his ridiculous turquoise jinni shoes with the curled up toes that came to a point. He wore a badge that said "staff." The pockets of his linen pants bulged. He reached into the right pocket and pulled out a wad of twenties the size of a soft ball. "Look who they trust with the money," he said.

"What would you do with more money?" said Diosa. "You're rich."

"I suppose you're right," said Serum. "I could steal some on principle."

"You don't have any principles," I said.

"Okay, then let's smoke a joint," Serum said.

"Here?" said Diosa.

"Somewhere else?" I said.

So we sat down on the ground and lit up. It was really good pot. My head swam and I passed out. I woke up a little. Serum and Diosa dragged me into the shade under the oak tree. Serum had a bottle of water and he poured water on my forehead. I stared up into the branches of the live oak, into the blue, blue sky. I felt pale. It was crowded. Serum and Diosa had to sit near my head as people walked by so they wouldn't kick me.

"He did this at a party," Diosa said to Serum. "Me and Mingo had to drag him out of the hot tub so he wouldn't drown. Remember? The tub was on the bottom deck then. We had to drag him naked step by step all the way up to the bedroom."

"I left my body," I said.

"You were fucking heavy," said Diosa.

"I was visiting my ancestors," I said.

"You were no help," Diosa said.

"I couldn't help. I wasn't there," I said.

"Are you here now?" said Serum.

"You don't choose when," I said. A wave of cold came over me.

"Pour some more water on him," Serum said.

I couldn't help thinking that I should lie on my back in the middle of crowds more often. The water felt good. The dirt beneath me turned to mud. I felt the cool mud up to my eyes as I stared past people's legs and into the waving branches that etched onto the blue, blue sky. I was going to pass out again. Maybe I'd passed out again already.

Suddenly Jesus was there.

"A guy wants to make a movie of you, Father," she said.

I looked across the way where stood a tall, thin, very pale fellow dressed all in white.

"He's making a movie about immortality. I told him you're the guy to talk to."

"He just wants my hat in his movie," I said.

I often wore a straw cowboy hat with lots of feathers in it, feathers I picked up on the trail as I rode: vulture feathers, red shouldered hawk feathers, dove feathers, an owl feather, pigeon feathers, raven feathers, red tailed hawk feathers, a pelican feather that I found on the beach in Malibu, one California Condor feather that Diosa and Jesus found for me in Big Sur; I sure had a lot of feathers; and people loved that hat; they loved it in Paris, they loved it in Prague, they loved it in Kathmandu. They love it in Malibu. It's been in fashion shoots, TV commercials.

"You should do it," said Diosa. "He knows a lot about immortality," she said to the tall, white man. We were standing in front of him now.

It must have been my movie month because I'd just interviewed for a documentary called *The Death of Writing in America*. Two young guys did that.

"Why me?" I asked them.

"Because you're famous?" said the director, Miko Shay, an Irish red head.

"I'm not."

"Because you're smart and funny!" said the other guy, Marco Polo, a dark Italian.

"I'm not that funny," I said.

"We shoot for ten hours, we use a few minutes."

"You're a good story teller," said Miko.

"I hate stories," I said.

"Your familiarity just bred contempt," said Marco.

"Will it make me rich and famous?" I said.

"It will make you immortal," Miko said.

Then I got a call from the people making *Children of Men*.

"We were told you were an expert," said the woman.

"Expert what?"

"On dystopia."

"I don't know very much, I just read them."

"That'll do."

I showed up at the studio and went through make-up. It took me a half-hour of filming to realize all they wanted me to do was repeat their questions as answers. "Do you think movies about dystopias are going to be the next thing?" "I think movies about dystopias are going to be the next thing," I said. Anyway, they hadn't read the book and didn't know the difference between post-apocalypse and dystopia. Neither did the movie.

Now this very tall, very white bald fellow dressed all in white picked me out of the teeming crowd and wanted to interview me about immortality. "This will be good for you," Diosa said. "You need the practice."

"For my movie or for immortality?" I said.

"A movie is immortality," Diosa said.

"Books?"

"Don't kid yourself," said Diosa.

"You should interview her," I said to the white fellow.

"I want you."

"I think movies about immortality will be the next thing," I said.

The white fellow turned with a wave and Diosa dragged me by the hand, past the beer booth to a cameraman who pointed a big camera at a young woman who sat on a big rock under a little tree. The woman had long black hair that swept behind her bare shoulders and she spoke to the camera, leaning back on her hands, tan legs stretched out, breasts forward, like a mermaid. "I want to live forever," she said.

"We represent the Oxford University Program for the Study of the Future," said the white fellow.

"You can't you study the future, it hasn't happened yet," I said.

"It's happening this very moment," said white fellow.

"This is the present," I said.

"The technology exists right now that will transform everything. Everybody alive right now will be able to live forever," white fellow said.

"Even if they don't want to?" said Diosa.

"Everyone wants to," said white fellow.

"I'd like to be about twenty years younger when I live forever," said Diosa.

"You will be! The technology exists!" white fellow said.

"Where?" I said.

"England."

"They can't even build a car," I said.

"Or fix a leak," said Diosa.

"The Japanese already have robots who can do everything for us!" said white fellow.

"I think that's the South Koreans," I said.

"So we'll all live forever with nothing to do?" said Diosa.

"Heaven!" said white fellow.

"Have you heard of The Talking Heads?" said Diosa.

"You don't think it will be a bit crowded?" I said.

"Wouldn't you want that for your children?" white fellow said.

"Where did Jesus go?" I said.

"I'd like my dog to live forever," said Diosa.

"Not your daughter?" said Jesus who seemed to appear again out of nowhere.

"You'll have it," white fellow said. "No poverty, starvation, illness. Humans will live like gods."

"All of them?" I said. I scratched my stubbled chin. I looked at Diosa. "I don't want to do this," I said to her.

"Just fucking do it, Shark," said Diosa.

"Yes," said white fellow. "Just do it!"

"Even in polytheisms the gods are only immortal *in sitio*," I said to him. "They don't survive their cosmos. For the Mesoamericans that could be as brief as fifty-two years. In some Hindu stories like the *Puranas*, immortality is a boon that Brahma gives to individuals after years of their practicing austerity, but every time it's given the person turns into a horrible demon who tortures gods and humans alike until everybody begs Shiva or Visnu to kill him."

"I told you he knew stuff," said Jesus.

"No, tyrants will be eradicated. Everyone will rise up to crush them," said white fellow.

"Like they do now," I said.

"Yes!" said white fellow.

"And what else will they do?" said Diosa.

"We'll all fall in love. Because love is the only thing faster than the speed of light," said white fellow.

"I like that all right," said Diosa.

I felt Diosa's forehead. I looked at white fellow. "That's just silly," I said.

"I made up the speed of light part," said white fellow.

"No shit," said Diosa.

"What do you want me to do?" I said.

"Just sit on that rock."

"There's somebody on that rock."

"When they're done!" white fellow said.

"You going to ask me questions?"

"Just talk about what you'd like to do once you're immortal," said white fellow.

I looked around. I looked back at white fellow. "I'd like to get rid of all these other assholes," I said. "It's hard enough being around them temporarily."

Me and white fellow had a very brief, quiet moment.

"Face your fear," he said.

"You're just some fucking Scientologist," I said to him. Then I took Diosa's hand and turned away. "I don't want to do it," I said.

"They wouldn't use anything you'd say anyways," said Diosa.

I shifted my eyes and found Serum's Dravidian face looking down at me.

"I'm back," I said.

"You're back all right," said Diosa. "Where'd you go this time?"

33

"Want more water?" said Serum.

"I have to pee," I said.

"So what?" Serum said.

Diosa took my hand and felt my forehead. "You're cold," said Diosa.

"I have to pee really bad and I can't stand up," I said.

"We can't carry you," said Diosa.

"I could have been immortal and instead I'm going to piss my pants."

"You piss your pants here and you'll be remembered for quite awhile," said Diosa.

Quite awhile. Maybe that would do.

ASK THE DUST

FRIDAY NIGHT, Diosa and I were coming back from dinner at Serum's when I noticed my pickup truck wasn't where I'd parked it. I never park it on top my front steps. Big yellow sticker on the window, big dent on the truck bed, back axle bent. The cab looked okay. There was hope. The perpetrator was drunk in a red Jeep. He tried to drive away, but he'd wrecked his Jeep. Tried to run away, but fell down. The CHP found him in my driveway. Poet Dan was there and saw it all.

"Kind of ironic, ain't it," said Poet Dan.

"What's ironic about it?" said Diosa.

"Everything," said Poet Dan. "It's Cinco de Mayo. It was a white guy."

"That's pretty fucking ironic," I said.

I called the CHP. I called my insurance. I called for a tow truck.

"No way on this weekend," said the dispatcher.

"You mean every tow driver in this town is Mexican?" I said.

"Do I have to answer that?"

We live at the end of a curve. When we first moved in here our neighbor was Tedso Blogunesky who was once the Polish surf champion. He was born in Malibu but his grandmother was Polish and he got citizenship. Better a champion in Poland than a nobody in Malibu. Now he was mostly stoned, but he married an older woman, a real estate agent, and he surfed everyday.

He used to park in front of our place until I asked him to move so I could park my truck there.

"I wouldn't park there if I was you," he said. He had long hair and a full beard.

"You park there."

"I'm not you."

"It's too hard pulling out backwards onto the road from my drive," I told him. Especially with two cars packed into it. You had to pull straight out. Cars come around a blind curve at fifty. They don't slow down, they just honk. You don't think of this stuff when you buy a place.

"You think that now," he said. "See that van?" He had a brown VW, old style, surf board on top, mysteriously parked in front of his place now. "It's my fifth one in five years."

I figured he just wanted my parking place. Turned out he was right. I made arrangements to have my truck towed on Monday and Diosa and Jesus made a big sign and taped it on my truck. It said SLOW DOWN!

"What do we do now?" I said.

"Get drunk and wait," said Diosa.

"For?"

"The next disaster."

It didn't take long. The next night the house shook, the dogs barked for an hour.

"Do you want to check that out?" said Diosa.

"I'm too sad," I said. "It's just an earthquake. Or the space shuttle landing."

"The dogs are still barking."

"If they get past the dogs, then there's Jesus, then me."

In the morning when I took out the recycling, my truck was in two pieces, one at the top of my steps and the other through the fence and on top my collapsed deck. Poet Dan was at the bottom of the steps reading my morning paper.

"Don't even say it," I said to him.

He folded up the Sports page and put it back in the paper. "Just checkin' the weather," he said.

"It's not going to rain for six months."

"Us homeless have to keep an eye on the weather," he said. "Have you tried that new Pinot at the Trader Joe's?"

Anyway, somebody came around the bend, lost control and smashed right into the SLOW DOWN! sign. He hit the tree just beyond so hard he tore the top off his car. That's how they found him. Drunk.

"Drinko de Mayo," said Diosa.

"How did we sleep through that?"

"We were drunk?" said Diosa.

I woke Jesus up. "How did you sleep through that?"

"I thought it was the space shuttle."

"The dogs barked," I said.

"The dogs always bark."

"Look on the bright side," said Diosa.

"There's a bright side?"

"In ten years it'll be a funny story."

I called my friend Bob who was a lawyer. He ran the American Oceans Campaign for Ted Danson. Back then I kept my mare, Jackie O, at his ranch just around the bend.

"Do I get my truck replaced twice?" I asked him.

"You'll be lucky to get it replaced once with depreciation."

"What about my deck?"

"Home insurance. Good luck."

"Can I sue somebody?"

"You'd need a lawyer."

"You?"

"You can't afford me. Two letters and you'd rub out the value of your truck. You riding your horse today?"

"I'm going to be busy," I said.

"This is really hilarious if you think about it," said Bob.

"You think about it. I don't want to think about it."

"It could only happen to you. I mean, who else could this kind of thing happen to?"

"You mean I made this happen."

"You have to think about it cosmically," said Bob. "How does anything happen? Just promise me I'll be in there when you write about it."

"You'll be in there all right."

"Use my real name. Go ahead," said Bob. "I have to get off now. Ted and I are practicing dying. Then we have to move on to our sex addiction."

The pieces of my truck had to be towed away on a flatbed.

"Think they'll total it?" I said to the driver, Carlos. I was trying to be funny.

"You should drive more carefully," he said to me.

"I was parked."

"You should park more carefully."

"Twice," I said. I told him what happened.

"It's a sign, you know," said Carlos, "from God."

Just find me somebody in this town who doesn't have a cosmic hotline.

The home insurance appraiser, Ward, wore a gray button down shirt with "Ward" in red script on the pocket. He held a clipboard. He took pictures with his phone. He had a kind, thoughtful face. "I don't know, it looks like this deck would have collapsed someday anyway," he said to me.

"Everything will collapse someday anyway," I said.

"But your deck collapsed now, is that what you're trying to say?" said Ward. He had gray fuzzy hair that he combed over his baldness.

"When my truck was knocked into it by a drunk."

"The wind could have knocked it down," Ward said. "Look at it."

"A truck was thrown on it," I said.

"So why was your truck in front of the deck?"

"It got knocked there by another drunk the night before."

"And you just left it there. Now you want us to be responsible."

"It was an accident. You're my insurance company."

"This looks like a car insurance problem, not a house insurance problem," said Ward.

"My car insurance will cover this?"

"I doubt it," Ward said.

My terrier, Piccolo, ran up and stood next to us. "Arf," said Piccolo.

"An over-aggressive dog," said Ward, the insurance guy. "I'll have to write you up for that."

"You're not going to give me any money?" I said.

"I'll give you a thousand."

"My deductible is a thousand," I said. "I've paid you guys tens of thousands over the last decades."

Ward the insurance claim man shrugged. "Productivity," he said.

My older brother, Gil, who just got laid off by *GE*, explained productivity to me that night on the phone.

"It was our operating concept," said Gil. "It's when you pay for something and we never have to give it to you. 100% profit. That's productivity. That's insurance, warranties, you name it."

"Do you think the cosmos has something to do with that, Gil?" I said.

"I'm in Pennsylvania. We don't do cosmos," said Gil

Now I had to reshuffle my debt to rebuild my deck. I hired a famous Argentinean Topanga handyman named George.

"So what would you like?" said George.

"Put it back together."

"Look," said George, "there is almost nothing here now. Think of the possibilities."

"I'm thinking of the debt, George."

"There will always be debt," said George. "We could double the size of your house. We could build up and up. Look, there, another terrace. Underneath your other deck, a beautiful, cavernous underground like Kubla Khan."

"I can't rebuild my whole house," I said.

"You can," said George. "Have a vision. Don't be afraid to take things apart and create."

And so George began to take things apart, decks, railings, fences, even my destroyed deck. But in the middle of taking my old deck apart a gray-haired woman in a canvas hat appeared amid the rubble.

"Hello," I said. "Can I help you?"

"What do you think you're doing?" she said.

"Rebuilding my deck?"

"You're on my property!" said the canvas-hatted woman. "Get off my property."

I looked in the opposite direction, across the debacle of my decks to where Clea and Radio's house sat, a foot over my property line.

"This is Topanga," I said to her gently. "This house was built in 1923. Everybody is on somebody else's property."

"Get off my property!" screamed the gray-haired canvas-hatted woman who stood on my disemboweled deck. She pointed to the vacant lot next door, a hillside acre of grass, dirt, oaks, boulders, yuccas, some cacti that I'd planted there when I ran out of room on my lot. I even had some cats buried there. "You've ruined my property! You've thrown dust and dirt on my property!"

"Dust?"I said.

She pointed to where some gravel and soil had spilled from my deck foundation.

"I'll move it," I said.

"Don't touch it!" said the woman. "It's mine now. Where did those boulders come from?"

I didn't know where the boulders came from. I never thought about where boulders came from. Boulders weren't really a *from* kind of thing. "The Jurassic?" I said.

"You have littered my property with boulders. And weeds! And oak tree debris!"

"Who are you?" I said.

"How long have you been here?" said the woman.

"Fifteen years," I said. "Who are you?'

"I'm not giving my identity to a criminal! I'm one of the owners of this land!" screamed the woman. "I know where the property line is!" She pointed to a spot about fifteen feet inside my deck foundation. "I own half your driveway!" the woman screamed.

"You own half of my house?"

"I'm just starting," said the canvas-hatted woman.

I looked around for George, but George was hiding under the picnic table.

"What's he doing under there?" the woman said.

"Hiding from you," I said.

"Well he's not doing a very good job," the woman said.

"Where were you fifteen years ago when I bought this place?" I said. "In fact," I said, finally gathering myself, "where have you been for the last fifteen years?"

"Get off my property!" screamed the woman standing on my broken deck. "Get off my property! Get off my property!"

George stayed under the picnic table until late in the afternoon, but when he came out I caught him.

"George, what are we going to do?" I asked.

"I am running away," said George. "But if nothing happens in a few months I'll come back and build all over her land."

"Is that part of our vision?"

"If your house is already on her land, then what's the difference?" said George.

But the next day a coven of canvas-hatted witches came from the vacant lot and peered over my broken fence, chattering and pointing and saying "property-property-property-line-line-property" and pointing at my hot tub and mumbling and then shouting, "Property! Property!"

"My God!" said Diosa. "We're being invaded by the characters from *On Golden Pond*!"

"You're a woman," I said. "You're diplomatic. Go talk to them."

"For you, my love, anything," Diosa said.

And so Diosa stepped outside. But before she could utter a word she was covered by a flurry of canvas hats and chattering, as if the chickens of hell had descended. She emerged, momentarily, went down again, then, disheveled, made a dash for daylight. I opened the door for her.

"They want us to move the hot tub and park somewhere else. They say you ruined their cactus garden."

"I planted the cactus garden!"

"I'm going shopping," Diosa said. "Be a man, Shark," she said. "I expect you to be a man."

I got on the phone to the only other lawyer I knew, my ex-student, Wil Deeth, now the head of the Los Angeles Sheriff's Department Law Office.

"Do nothing," said Wil.

"You going Zen on me, Wil? Help me out."

"I'm too powerful to help you," said Wil Deeth. "It would look like a conflict of interests."

"What can I do?"

"Endure," said Wil. "Do nothing."

The next day the first witch returned with a truckload of men. They wore black t-shirts with MAYA written across the chest. They unloaded from the bed of the little white truck and began shoveling dirt into it. The wicked witch pointed. "You'll not get my land!" she screamed at me. "You'll get no more of my land!" She jumped into her truck and drove away with the dirt. The Maya workers piled on top the mound which, but for the tiny size of the truck, looked like a small version of Popocatepetl surrounded by squatting giants. Then she returned with the truck empty but for the Maya and shooed them into the field, pointing, directing, as they shoveled and picked, attacked the earth for another load of dirt. Again and again they left and returned, their clinking shovels resounding.

"What are they doing?" Diosa said.

"She's moving her land," I said.

"And then what, Father?" said Jesus.

"And then she'll move ours."

I saw the chagrin in his Jesus' eyes. In Diosa's the look of panic and desperation. Could we endure?

(A DESCENT INTO SPIDER WORLD)

I journeyed into Spider World, the crawl space beneath my house where *everything lost* was stored, a place of deep and horrible memory: old toys, pictures, journals, letters from old girl friends, broken cameras, photo albums, ancient technologies like land line telephones and stereo equipment, electronic drum rhythm machines, stuffed toy animals, last year's taxes, Christmas ornaments, waterbeds, paint cans, gardening tools, exotic wine, extension cords, fertilizer, paint cans, old rugs, the skeletons of dead mammals, whole segments of peoples' lives, some dead, some living, the arms and legs of one story, the torso of another, disembodied personalities, ghosts, and most of all, spiders! which hung from the rotting rafters in sheets and galaxies of gauze white webbing, the air woven in silver, faces in the webs between the black or ephemeral bodies of black bodied spiders and long legged spiders. No one would go in there but me and even for me it had to be sacred search, a dire search, a dire Orpheus-like search.

There, I searched out Jesus' video cassette tape of *The Wizard of Oz*. I emerged. I found the sequence where the Wicked Witch of the West appears. It said, da-da-da-dunt-da-dah-dunt, da-da-da-dunt-da-dah-dunt. I put my stereo speakers out the window and played it every time the canvas-hatted witch reappeared.

"This is action? said Diosa, holding her ears.

Ands she was right, it did no good. Soon, all the dirt from the vacant lot would be gone, the hillside would be gone, trees, cacti, bushes, even boulders, rubbed out, and then, then when all that was left was the frail wreckage of my deck, it too would be stacked into the back of the white truck, half my cement driveway battered to dust and carted away, my retaining wall eviscerated, and then my foundation, my house crumbling down from above, crumbling helplessly onto the vacant lot where my life and the lives of my loved ones would be carted away in the back of the little white truck, my canvas-hatted neighbor cackling.

I watched as they began rolling boulders down the hill. Heard them whacking at the elephantine stone that held up my retaining wall. "Wil! Wil!" I said aloud, "I am nothing! I'm doing nothing, but nothing in the face of everything!"

"My property! My property!" I heard from the hill, beneath the grunts of the Maya who once built cities from these kinds of stones, but now lifted the boulders into the white truck with ka-thunk and clang. They drove away. Returned. My property. My property, I thought with great irony. The canvas-hatted woman leapt upon the top of her cab. She spotted me in my window. "I'll have it all!" she shouted. "I just want you to be a good neighbor! I just want you to respect the property line!" Then, beneath the clang of shovels, came the tick-tick of a pick-ax. The Maya workers spread in a line across the hill, once florid with wildflowers and now barren, the dust rising in clouds. Tick-tick. Tick-tick. Then, suddenly, the men put down their picks and shovels. They turned their palms up to the screaming canvas-hatted visage. She stood, waving her arms frantically at me who turned on my sound track to *The Wizard of Oz*. I strode outside. I stood on my rubble. The workers had hit mountainside. Nothing more could be removed. The assault was over.

The witch was defeated at her own game. I saw the leaden relief fall from the flattened shoulders of the Maya who laid down their picks and shovels and walked together to the French café down the street, emerging moments later with iced espressos and croissants.

The woman turned on me. "I'll be back," she said, and even so, the next morning, brought a canvas-hatted gringo with a jack-hammer and an Hispanic boy, he looked Honduran, with a white, plastic bucket. She followed as the man lugged the machine up the hill, its wicked tail trailing back to an electrical generator in the back of the truck. The machine rattled against the mountain, but in time I recognized that the chatter was only a staccato version of the tick-tick I'd heard yesterday. Tick-tick-tick-tick-tick-tick-tick-tick. After two hours they'd gathered enough dust to fill the bucket and the Honduran boy carried it down to the truck. The woman held her left hand on her forehead under her canvas hat. She had the man and boy put the generator on the ground, then she drove away with the bucket of dust. The man and the boy went for an espresso.

By day's end, there was only the bare mountain, the jack-hammer sprawling like an exhausted dragon, the remnants of picks and shovels strewn like bones across the hill. And in the coming days arrived the men in orange vests carrying tripods and lenses, mirrors bouncing light, and men, who could see each other perfectly clearly, shouting and waving like lost mountain climbers. I walked across my rubble and into the devastated landscape. I spotted a man in a yellow, plastic helmet near the top of the hill where a little of my fence still stood.

"Can I help you?" I said.

"I doubt it," the man said.

"Are you looking for the line?"

"There are no lines here," the man said. "Why should there be any lines here?"

"Then what are you doing?" I asked.

"Looking for the line," said the man.

They came again. They came for days and days and then they stopped. That's where things stood. In time, George returned. He put some things back together. He worked very slowly and for weeks it seemed as if things had only fallen apart worse, but just as I'd decide to fire him, a lone wall might appear, or the intimation of a deck. "Look," George said, pointing south to the vacant lot next door. "Have you thought about a cabana and a swimming pool? Look, there," he said, pointing behind my house to some property claimed by the neighbor above. "I think we could put in a garden and an astronomical observatory. A bamboo grove. A meditation room." I glanced at my shack of a house and the surrounding rubble that spread beneath the giant oak in front. I looked out upon the land beyond. Here, in Los Angeles, every handful of dust was worth a million dollars. It seemed a world full of infinite possibility.

AT THE UNIVERSITY
OF LA-LA HOLY

"PROFESSOR SHARK?" said a small voice on my phone. "My name is Rhonda Riordon and you are my advisor because you do the R's?"

"How did you get my number?" I said.

"It says on my red advisee sheet—do you have my red sheet?"

"Why would I have your red sheet if you have your red sheet?"

"Because my name is Rhonda Riordon and you are my advisor because you do the R's?"

"What do you need to know?" I asked.

"It says here on my red sheet that I have to take both one course in English literature before 1800 and one after? Does that mean I have to take one course in English literature before 1800 and one after?" asked Rhonda.

"Would you accept yes as an answer?" I said.

"Both? Not one or the other?"

"What do you think *both* means?" I asked.

"One or the other?"

"It means both," I said,

"I mean," said Rhonda, "maybe they're saying both, but they mean one or the other."

"Who are *they*," I said. "Who do you think *they* are?"

"I don't know," said Rhonda. "That's a good question. That could be something important to think about."

"What do you mean when you say *both*?" I asked.

"That's a good question, too," said Rhonda. "Maybe I would mean one or the other. It would certainly be better for me if it meant one or the other."

"Well, Rhonda Riordon," I said, "as your advisor I advise you to think that it means that you have to take one of each."

"Oh, I was afraid of that," Rhonda said. "Maybe I shouldn't have called. Do you know when 1800 is?"

"When?" I said.

"I mean, how do I know what's before and what's after?" said Rhonda in her small voice.

I tried to remain calm. After all, it was only my life I was wasting here and one needed to, if not enjoy it, at least concentrate on it, with detachment. "Anything from 1799 and lower is before," I said. "1800 and up is after."

"So like the Twentieth Century is after?" asked Rhonda.

"That's right."

"The Nineteenth?"

"After," I said.

"And the Eighteenth is after then, right?" Rhonda asked.

"The Eighteenth Century is the 1700's," I said. "It's before."

"The Eighteenth Century is the 1700's! Oh my God!" said Rhonda Riordon. "How can that be? Is that why everything is divided at 1800? Why do you people do that?"

"*Us* people?"

"Then there's this thing with fiction and nonfiction. How can something be *non* and true. Shouldn't fiction be about true stuff and nonfiction be made up?"

"Often it is," I said. "Maybe you should be a philosophy major."

"Do you think?" Rhonda asked.

"Yes," I said, "then you could get a philosophy advisor."

"But you are my advisor, Professor Shark. How can seventeen be called eighteen?"

"One to ninety-nine is the First Century," I said.

"No!"

"Yes."

"Well that's the problem then," said Rhonda Riordon.

"Indeed," I said. I couldn't ever remember having said *indeed* before. Anyway, it went on like that for quite some time.

> Calm covers peaks.
> Among the treetops
> A breath hangs like a leaf.
> In the deep woods
> Birdsong sleeps.
> At the foot of hills
> Slopes find their peace.
> Be patient. Wait.
> Soon, you too, will cease.

I, JESUS: THE LIFE OF
JESUS IN LOS ANGELES

MORNING IN TOPANGA. Is it ten years ago? Things change. Things
stay the same. Finches and orioles are in the trees. My cat, Mucha Plata, brings
a live mouse into the living room, five kittens following on her tail. I let her out
onto the deck where she puts the mouse in the food bowl. The mouse, on his
hind legs, stares at the kittens. The kittens stare back. The mouse jumps out of
the food bowl, races to the porch railing and leaps twenty feet to the ground
below. A mouse suicide. But then it stirs, staggers to its feet. Another cat,
Music Batty, snatches it up. What would Walt Disney say?

I sat down and put cream cheese on half a bagel. The LA Times still
existed and I glanced at the Sports page. The Angels were playing the Giants
in the World Series. Notre Dame was winning again. UCLA was handing
out handicap parking cards to its football players. Diosa read everyone's
horoscope. Great things were about to happen for me. Diosa was to have
a lover from a foreign land. My daughter, a nascent teenager, was to take
advantage of a great opportunity. She wandered into the room and sat down
at the table. Her hair was like fire.

"How can horoscopes change everyday, given the relative non-motion
of the stars?" I said for the thousandth time. "Doesn't this stuff take a little
time to work itself out?"

"Don't be a jerk," said Diosa.

"Yes, Father, don't be a jerk," my daughter said.

The mother cat, Mucha Plata, was behind us now, at the window. She'd caught a bird, taken it over the roof and behind the house, walked along the top of the fence, crossed the deck, and now sat on the deck railing, a three foot leap to the window.

"Burddurpertle?" she said.

"No birds in the house," I said.

"Can I have the cream cheese?" asked my daughter. "I'm changing my name to Jesus."

"Great," I said.

"Do you think it will affect my grades?"

"Yes."

"Because, I've been thinking about it, and I am Jesus," said my daughter.

"Keep it to yourself," said Diosa.

"Everybody is Jesus," I said.

"No, I'm Jesus," said my daughter.

"And I am your father," I said.

"Unfortunately you cannot be my father, Father," Jesus said. "God is my father. You're that, you know, that other guy."

"Joseph," said Diosa.

"Yes," said Jesus. "Joseph."

"I remember when you were Luke Skywalker," I said.

"I was seldom Luke Skywalker," Jesus said.

"It's a logical transition," I said. "Luke, I am your father."

"Mother, request that he shuts up," Jesus said to Diosa.

"Your mother is the Virgin Mary?" I said.

"Yes," said Diosa.

"Thank you, Mother," said Jesus.

"And God?" I said.

"Lives down the street?"

"Everywhere?" I said.

"Precisely," said Jesus. "This isn't going to be easy at first. People hate it when Jesus shows up."

Mucha Plata was back on the porch with the bird. Must have come down from the roof. I got up and let the kittens out again. Mucha Plata put the bird in the food bowl and this time the kittens attacked its breast while four adult cats watched.

"I guess everybody knows what a bird is," Diosa said.

"And what a food bowl is," I said. "And what food is. Jesus Christ."

"Yes?" said Jesus.

One of the dogs, Piccolo, began howling and ten seconds later I heard the kitchen door. Serum's daughter, Ashley, came up the stairs.

"I knew she was coming," Jesus said. "I'm becoming prescient."

"It's my week to drive," I said.

"That changes nothing," said Jesus. "I knew. I'm Jesus," she said to Ashley.

"Cool," said Ashley.

"This isn't starting off that badly," said Jesus.

"Could you get me a new iPad?" said Ashley.

"I don't do iPad's. You'll have to talk to God."

"Wouldn't he already know?" Ashley said.

"He does, but you still have to ask," said Jesus.

"It's time to go," I said.

How would Los Angeles handle another coming of Christ?

The ride to school went pretty quietly, four miles down the canyon to the coast, then along the PCH for a couple miles to Temescal Canyon. Jesus put on her make-up using the sun visor mirror. Off shore, pelicans dove for fish, a pod of dolphins lazily wove the surface. Jesus pointed out the Christian bumper stickers. "My people," she said. "They're everywhere."

GABRIELA

GABRIELA SAT AT a computer in front of a window larger than a prison cell. At the university. Some new hell. When La-La Holy moved into this new building Gabriela had no seniority so her department chair put her in a small, windowless office on the inside hallway. But after her years of confinement she feared she'd go crazy in there. They put her in there anyway. She went crazy anyway. Her hair fell out again. It made La-La Holy look lousy. The dean changed her office but it was bad politics for her promotion and tenure. Good thing she was a famous Latina refugee.

Now she could see everything. To her left, beyond Lincoln Boulevard, the remaining patch of the Ballona Wetlands, once a marshland, then an oil field, now restored, kind of, the compromise for selling off the rest of it to developers: Playa Vista was nowhere near a beach; from Vista del Mar you couldn't see the ocean. My neighbor, Bob, negotiated the deal with the city. It was land already wasted by sulfur, the refuge of oil drilling, land returned to a state it had never been in. That's not ecology, it's deconstruction. Los Angeles is not about illusion, but creation.

Beneath the bluff on which the Hall of La-La Holy overlooked it all, once Howard Hughes had an airfield. He built the Spruce Goose there. When I first got to LA it was the Spruce Goose graveyard, empty runways and airplane hangars. I love ruins, especially contemporary ruins, Hollywood, the Salton Sea. Playa Vista's faux-Euro canned condos rise woodenly up, a kind of gay depression spread all packed in, each one special; and then beyond, Marina del Rey stretching to the ocean, a shoreline Gabriela can trace west and south to Malibu and Point Dume, then, with a turn of her head she can sweep across the southwestern slopes of the Santa Monica Mountains where Diosa and I live, somewhere; but she can never figure out exactly where; it just looks like a frozen sea, *mar de hielo*; funny, because the sea never freezes and there is the sea looking frozen and the ocean, which never freezes, and the mountains, a frozen sea running to it; she plays with that idea, the running permanence and iron fluidity, geography laced with poetry, politics, everything poetry and politics; under the slopes of those mountains the cities of west Los Angeles: Venice, Santa Monica, the Palisades, Culver City, Westwood, Century City, Beverly Hills, West Hollywood, Hollywood (on local radio addresses are given as if Los Angeles were a state, not Culver City, California, but Culver City, Los Angeles), their downtowns, business buildings clustered among spreading neighborhoods, break the horizon like, well, God forbid, like tombstones, and on a clear day she can even see the white HOLLYWOOD sign etched like a chalk line upon the hills.

Between the cities, the freeways flow into each other like veins and arteries, corpuscles, capillaries, the Marina Freeway, the San Diego Freeway, the Santa Monica Freeway, the Harbor Freeway, the new 105, the 605, the 710. Once, in Bahia Blanca, her birthplace in Argentina, when she was just a girl, she looked at a map of Los Angeles and tried to memorize the freeways and cities inside, all the freeways of the city most free of all the free cities of free America, but like freedom they were so abstract, and then she grew up and became a young woman with a child and found the elbows of America swinging too freely, the free hands of America taking food from her baby, the free press of America freely choosing to ignore thirty thousand of her comrades murdered; isn't it horrible what happens in other countries? And now she is here. Plucked out. She must learn how to drive. Mingo won't learn since he rolled a van in Seattle without a license. "They arrested me," he said. "I didn't have a license to roll a van." But me and Diosa will get tired of carting her and her family around. We live twenty miles away.

Beneath the bluff, the rumble of steam shovels and bulldozers like Tonka Toys in a sand box, constructing Vista del Mar, and to the right of that, the last remaining runways and hangars of the Hughes Airport. The Hall of La-La Holy was once the Hughes Technology Building, home of Reagan's Star Wars research, four stories high and four deep. When everybody got their new offices, Gabriela and Mingo, me and Diosa, the four of us and our kids, Jesus and Eva and Anahi, sneaked into the building through a construction entrance and purified the offices, burning white sage we'd gathered in Topanga on the Santa Maria Trail; Jesus played the sitar, the girls recited poems, a bottle of wine for each room (the kids went off and rolled round coffee tables down the silent escalators), Diosa danced; we smoked pot (for Gabriela and Mingo, their first; in Argentina the Left didn't smoke pot or drop acid; drugs were bourgeois, a diversion from the cause; Mingo smoked a little that day, but couldn't tell if he was high, and Gabriela, just a puff), she watched us that day, her new friends, like many things, something forged before they'd thought it out, the fissures between the binding like the cleavage in young sandstone, like those mountains beyond, only twenty million years old, still sliding into the sea; where was the Left in America? I quoted Beckett to her: "Don't wait to be hunted to hide."

The Spruce Goose. What things men do. Two dilapidated airplane hangars still hunched at the end of the far runway as if waiting for something to hatch, like the baby caterpillars in *Mothra*, I'd told her. Would it be constructive or destructive, she asked me, to start thinking like me?

She let her mind stretch beyond the horizon to a beach she couldn't see, the Playa, and found Mingo there, his eyes as gray as the ocean, his mind incessant, his incessant heart, and now, when she awakens in midnight, she places her ear on his drunken chest, listens, and feels as if it were the last thing between her and the abyss. When she was nineteen, a university student in Bahia Blanca, she had a husband and a littler girl. Then soldiers came. How many guns does it take to arrest a nineteen year old girl and a baby? Hundreds. Thousands. It takes semi-automatic rifles, troop carriers, tanks, helmets and boots. It takes an army. It takes a nation.

She never saw her husband, Pablito, again though she saw his name years later on a list of the dead smuggled into the jail and passed from cell to cell through toilet pipes, whispered through sink drains, carried in your vagina or in your ass. Where was it that she found him dead? For two years she'd been blindfolded and chained to a wire bed. Twenty-five other women were in that barracks at the Little School. One was pregnant when she came in. Four more were pregnant when they left. Shot in the adjoining yard, thrown from planes, raped to death, starved to death, tortured to death until you felt nothing of them but their bones which cracked like chalk and their skin which lay over them like yellow wax paper. When she was the last they threw water on her bare metal bed springs and electrified it with a cattle prod. Then she envied the dead, the sweet dead who'd joined their husbands and lovers and friends but not their children. You never knew what happened to your children. It had been twenty-five years since she'd seen Rosalita, her baby girl.

Below her a steam shovel gullets red-brown dirt and waves its head at the sky. Where will the birds go? The herons and egrets, ducks and doves? The ten thousand things that once lay in the swamp. To where do they slither and crawl? Was there an Amnesty International for animals? Just go over there, to the new wetlands, cross twelve lanes of Lincoln Blvd., to the United States of New Wetlands, a place you've never been, where you don't speak the language, where you know no one. Oh thank you, thank you, for saving *my* life, because now it's all okay; the rest are dead, 30,000 dead, a hundred thousand dead, millions dead, millions more to come, but my life has been saved, so thank you God, thank you USA, thank you all you people in your demon automobiles. She ran a hand through her thick, brown hair. She could feel which ones were gray because they twisted and curled, and she'd lost it all too many times; it was beginning to thin at the top. She should talk to Diosa about it. She had to buy a car and learn to drive. You had to drive here. She should talk to me. Now the hills across the way look like pregnant women lying on their backs, like Teresita chained to the bed next to hers (she could see her through the space the blindfold left as it crossed over her nose), Teresita's belly swollen with the child of the guard they called *Comadrejito*, Little Weasel. Blindfolded, Teresita gave birth on the same metal bed where Comadrejito electrocuted her and raped her. Blindfolded, Gabriela brought the baby boy out with her free hand, chewed the cord, tore away her own rags to wrap the child who Teresita bore and birthed but never saw because the next morning they came and took it and the next day they shot Teresita in the yard.

Eventually, one day, someone comes and you are taken. The sun sets no matter how long you linger. You can count your sorrows or your blessings all the way to the grave. Here, the city of angels lies beneath the blue, blue sky. Below, the ever-drier wetlands rumble. There is a moment when the earth is giddy. It feels as if a train is in the office and she places her hands on her desk to steady herself as the concrete beneath her rolls and everything heaves to a stop. In the old airplane hangar, from the dark, two lights appear, simultaneously blinking, like lanterns, like flashlights, like eyes, like stars, like eyes.

SEA MINGO

SEE MINGO. See Mingo run. He is running to the ocean. The ocean is to the west. Now the ocean is to the west when once the ocean was to the east. Once it was the Atlantic Ocean he ran to, now it is the Pacific. Lots of things were different then. Winter came in June. He was a boy, skipping school. Then a young man who thought the world could be changed and the difference between good and evil was knowledge and ignorance.

From the top of the hill, the homes of the Playa stretch down to the sea, white stucco and red, clay roofs against the turquoise blue. To the south, over the sanitation plant in El Segundo, planes roar over LAX, two out and two in, every thirty seconds, and the roar of the ocean and the stink of sanitation and the blue of the sea and the sucking of an airplane toilet pops and sucks like ocean riptide sucking over black rocks on the shore.

In a year or two I'll take him to Pfeiffer Sate Beach, Big Sur, and he'll sit on a ragged rock at the ocean shore, before the eye of a black cave blinded in white surf, the ocean pouring at him, its white hands grabbing the black shore, and as it sucks back over the rocks, popping like machine gun fire, he sees the bodies of his compañeros lying in the foam, round black rocks like boots, like skulls, shoulder blades arching from their shallow graves while here, in Los Angeles, where they burned everyone living and dead and made them smoke and made them sky, he pauses at the sea where below him, beneath the crests of waves collapsed in heaves straight and vicious against the sand, the boats of the dead unload. *Montoneros. Montoneros. Montoneros.*

Now we're sitting in my house, the four of us, Gabriela, Diosa, Mingo, and me. The dawn is threatening and the soldiers take him outside and put him against a wall. Does he want a blindfold? No, he wants to look at them. They raise their guns. They put them down. They put him back in isolation. Raise your glass, he says to us, and we toast, Salud.

Last Saturday night at 3 a.m. below the Santa Monica Pier, his new friend, me, stripped and threw himself into the surf under a full moon, a sky white with moon glow, and Gabriela gazed upon a naked man, a flying dolphin, the rush of surf; she ran her fingers dancing upon Mingo's shoulders like the tentacles of some ocean thing and said, "Look, his ass is like the moon."

Moments before, when they stood together in the warm wind, Diosa walked shoeless to the curling surf and turned to me yelling, "It's glorious, you'll have to go in!" Now she stood with Mingo and Gabriela on shore watching me, my brown back and white gold moon butt flying into waves. The white light moonlight beamed narrow light. The night air fell like whispers, the sky silken, the sand like the fur of a hound. Gabriela stood behind him and pushed her thumbs into his shoulders. "You don't have to go in, *mi flaco*," she said. "You are the sun, not the moon." She ran her hands through his thick, gray hair, long, flowing over his shoulders and down his back, Porteño style, La Boca.

"I don't have to go in there," Mingo said. "Besides, he's crazy."

The water was black like a wall and I was black and the breaking waves like silver, like light, like lead bars, like stripes on the low sky; me flying between them.

"He's crazy, but he's a good swimmer," Mingo said.

Gabriela put her arm around Diosa's waist. "Do you ever wish to be young again?" she said.

"Without having to be young," Diosa said.

Once Mingo was young. Once he was a young husband with a young wife and two sons. Now they were dead. Now he stared across the white beach of Playa del Rey. The sky is almost yellow. He has an hour to run home and pick up his daughters from school. Behind him, at the park, some low riders gathered. Chicano rap pounded and rippled over the hot blacktop. They have their guns out, hanging from their hands, and the sun shines from the gun barrels like blue stars. Near them, kids play at a playground on blue plastic ladders and yellow slides, their voices trembling out beneath the rap like the call of birds upon the pond bulging at the end of this Venice Canal, the brown ducks and green-necked mallards with necks like gun barrels, a blue heron stands motionless, gulls swoon, a hummingbird flirts and dips at the flowering ice plants; in Argentina, his grandmother told him that hummingbirds rescued the souls of dead children as they lay in the calyx of a flower, lifting them with needle beak, flying them to the Land Without Evil.

He ran his hands through his hair and tied it back behind his head. He ran down the road to the beach, across the bike path, a quarter mile of white sand, the pounding shore where his eyes water freely where he can scream all he wants, when they pull out your fingernails, cut off fingers, put electrodes under his skin, beg for mercy? yes, tell them what you know? you tell them everything, things you know and things you don't; a man sat behind his head and wrote it down because they don't want screaming on tape, not even in kangaroo court; you are even better at telling them things you don't know. Once he wanted to change the world. He settled for trying to change his government. Then helping the poor. Then, if he could, the lives of his friends, his wife, his children, his own life, and finally he was given only the worst wish of all, his last.

Last weekend Gabriela took the girls to see the movie *The Search for El Dorado*, a cartoon. "How-how! Heap good movie!" Eva said.

"My great grandfather died on the plains of Uruguay, a Guarani, fighting the gauchos," he said to his daughter.

"Papi," said Anahi, "you're Italian!"

"A little bit Indian," he said.

"Look around you," Gabriela said to him. "The battle is lost."

It's 1998 in Los Angeles. His daughters dance in the living room, each to her own Disney Discman in front of a rap video on the giant screen, at their feet Sega Genesis, Nintendo 64, Disney Cube (soon the technology will be different, but they'll have all that, too); they want to go to the Santa Monica Pier, Universal City, the Promenade, Disneyland, Las Vegas; they want to marry a Back Street Boy, Eminem, Blink 182; they want to be Britney Speers.

Who brought these things, Mingo? You?

COLLAPSING WITH
THE STARS

"HOW ABOUT WRITING for the movies?" Diosa and I had just gotten teaching jobs in Los Angeles and a famous Hollywood screen agent, Augie Sands, had my phone number before our furniture arrived.

"I want to finish my next book," I said. "And learn to surf."

"What did they pay you for your book?" said Augie.

"$5,000."

"You could make that in a day," Augie Sands said to me.

"Everyday?"

"What's your salary?"

$50,000."

"A year?" he said. "You'd make that in a week. Add it up. Do you know how hard it is to live in this town on less than $500,000?"

"I don't go to the movies," I said.

"All the better. I see you don't have an answering machine. What do you type on?"

"A typewriter?"

"You're crazy," he said. "You're a caveman. But you wrote a funny book."

A week later he sent me an answering machine, a desktop computer, and the screenplay of a classic movie he'd represented, *Bull Durham*.

"What's it about?" said Diosa.

"Sex and baseball," I said.

"How original," she said. "Should we rent it?"

"No," I said. "Reading it was hard enough. Want to read it?"

"Can I skip the baseball?"

"They have sex while playing baseball," I said.

In a week I had an appointment to pitch a mini-series at HBO. It was on a movie lot. In the coming months, on the way to pitching movie ideas, I walked through the sets of America's dreams. Chinatown. Batman. Star Wars. Some Like It Hot. I shook the hands of a dozen stars I couldn't name. The HBO office was in a doublewide trailer on the lot of Fox or Paramount or MGM or Universal or somewhere. A kid in his twenties answered the door. "Great book," he said. He took me into a room where a guy in his forties sat behind a messy desk and talked on the phone. "This is Rosenthal," the kid said. The older guy gave a slight wave without raising his head, then went back to shuffling papers and talking.

"Tony Ackers," said the kid. It was some name like that. "He produces everything. Don't worry, he's listening. What was it like shooting heroin with those black guys?"

"I didn't do that," I said.

"It's in the book," he said.

"I made it up."

"Fiction isn't made up," he said. "It's autobiographical."

"My neighbor shooting cannon balls from his porch, that's true," I said.

"That's unbelievable," he said. "Have you seen *A Hitch-hikers Guide to the Galaxy?*"

"I read a little of the book," I said. The older guy had yet to look up.

"That's what I envision," the kid said.

"In my next book my hero is an interplanetary garbage man," I said to him.

"I don't like that," he said. "It doesn't work for me. Let me think about this and get back to you." We shook hands. Tony didn't say good-bye. I never heard from them again.

That happened a half-dozen times before I ended up in front of a woman executive at Fox who pretty much put me through the same thing minus the kid. She read scripts and talked on the phone while I pitched some of my ideas and she shook her head. "The world isn't ready for homosexual basketball players," she said without looking up. "Besides, we did a sports movie last year."

"Hasn't everything already been done?" I said. "Isn't it about the writing?"

With that, she actually looked at me. "Here's a movie idea. Give me four tits, two asses, and a funny guy in between. Can you write that?"

Was that an idea? I didn't know if I could write it. Why would I want to write that? Why would anyone want to write that? Why write it at all? Thinking about it, was there a person who actually wrote that stuff? Couldn't you just get four tits, two asses, and a funny guy and turn them loose in front of the camera? Isn't that what Larry David already did? Was there somebody better at writing that stuff than somebody else?

"Yes," said Augie. He'd agreed to meet Diosa and me at a bar on Sunset. "It's about the money. All great writing sells. Stick your genius in between the lines."

I figured that "between the lines" was an industry euphemism for some real place.

"Your pitching sucks," he said to me. "You're ruining my reputation."

Then Diosa walked in.

"Jesus Christ," he said. "With that on your arm you could sell anything."

So I went back out, this time with Diosa. And Augie was right. We did a lot better. You know, she was the brains and I was the beauty. We started getting call backs to develop our ideas. We sat in front of producers. There was always a pretty blonde or a cute boy to whom the producer said things like, "That sounds like a great part for George Clooney. Get him on the phone." The assistant left. Came back in. "Call Will Smith, then try Depp." After a few months of that I wasn't getting much of my own writing done, or surfing.

Then a producer's assistant called and asked us for our birthdays.

"How sweet," I said to Diosa. "We'll get birthday presents. You see? They're human!"

But Augie said our birthdays were used to check our horoscopes. There were bad omens and we were dropped.

"Check your horoscopes! Give fake birthdays!" said Augie.

"The learning curve is tough," I said.

Finally an actual producer from Paramount called. "I want the Mormon polygamy thing," he said.

"Okay, great," I told him.

"Write it up and send it to me."

"What am I writing up?"

"A screenplay."

"Don't we get paid?"

"Trust me," he said.

I never trust anybody who says "trust me." And at least Augie had already told us never to write anything before we were paid. I called him and told him we didn't want to pitch ideas anymore.

"Everybody in the world wants to be doing what you're doing," he said to me. "I meet dozens of novelists every month and all they want to do is be in Hollywood."

In the meantime, my agent in New York called and asked me how my next book was going.

"Poorly."

"How's life out there with the stars?" she said.

"I'm a white dwarf," I said.

"Is that better than a black hole?"

"I'd prefer to be a black hole," I said.

In Los Angeles, if you tell someone you're a writer, they want to know what movies you've written or what TV show you work on (TV shows are written in writing rooms, by committees). If you say you've been to a reading, they think you're seeing a psychic. The entertainment section of the LA Times runs everyday, with full page movie ads and dozens of reviews of TV shows and movies; some are reviewed again and again. Often more time is spent on how much money a movie makes than what happens in it. Movies based on books often do not mention the author and, if by chance someone alludes to a literary circumstance, they refer to the movie, not the book. And usually what they're referring to didn't happen in the book. The LA Times Book Review shares a small fold out section in the Sunday paper and only spits out a couple book reviews a week; usually it's a book about some celebrity.

So I figured I'd give the movies one more shot. Cowboy poetry was all the rage and Diosa and a friend of hers had written and published a literary send-up of two cowgirls corresponding to each other via cowgirl poems. I read a bunch of books on screenwriting, set the cowgirl book to plot points and wrote a screenplay, a romantic comedy. A screenplay based on a book of poems. I thought it was hilarious. Funnier and sexier than *Bull Durham*. I sent it to Augie. After two months I called him.

"Are you, crazy?" he said to me. "Nobody's going to pay twenty million for this."

"Twenty million?" I said. "How about twenty thousand?"

He hung up. He was through with me. But a friend of ours named Marla, who was also flirting with the industry, read my screenplay.

"It's idiosyncratic, but I'm sleeping with a Hollywood producer at Sundance," she said to me. "Let me give it to him."

"A Hollywood producer?" I said. "I thought Sundance was independent."

"Don't be a fool," she said. "You think they pay for it with bake sales?"

A week later I was a finalist at Sundance. A week after that Marla broke up with the producer. A week after that my screenplay was rejected by Sundance. That was some time ago. Since, a few of my novels have been optioned for movies, but I always refuse to write the screenplay. I tell them, "Take the book. Do what you want with it. The book is the book." And that's pretty much how I feel about it. I mean, have you ever seen a Hollywood movie and said, "Boy, I wish I'd written that!"

Living out here, I still run into screenwriters and directors and producers all the time. Inevitably they shake my hand and say, "I wish I'd chosen to do what you did."

And I say, "I wish I had your money."

But I don't think they could choose to do what I do, anymore than I could choose to do what they do. Hollywood is a world upside down from mine. Sometimes I write hundreds of pages to find an idea. I don't even use an outline, let alone a storyboard. Issues of depth and complexity aside, my writing process is completely different from that world, private, contemplative, and about words, not pictures.

All artists and writers live with market challenges, not just the ones who live in Los Angeles. And though the popular appeal of movies and television likely reflects the fact that people don't read, in the end movies and TV aren't our competition. Our competition is Garcia Marquez, Tolstoy, Virginia Woolf, Roberto Bolaño.

Which leads me to my last story. Some years back, when I was teaching introduction to fiction, a nineteen year old student of mine said to me, "Hey, I know you. I read one of your books."

"Which one?" I said.

"The one that's in New York now."

"The unpublished one I just finished?"

"Yeah," he said. He told me that before a New York editor could take a novel to the publishing house's marketing committee, they sent it to Hollywood where the studios hired readers to recommend whether or not the book would make a good movie. That was his job. In front of me stood my teenage student who had decided whether or not my book would be considered in New York.

"Did you like it?" I said.

"Nah," he said, "it didn't work for me."

A GOOD MAN IS
HARD TO FIND

THIS STARTS a while ago, in 2003, but it ends now.

In my class on Writing Dialogue filled with thousands of unregistered beings, I made everyone write a scene in which the characters were Jesus, Hitler, and Shakespeare. It was a disaster. No one could break the chains of decay, I mean cliché. Maybe I meant decay. Once, I forbade all references to Jesus, Hitler, or Shakespeare. Once, I demanded that all the arguments and examples for the whole semester must come from the lives of Jesus, Hitler, and Shakespeare. Once I taught the whole class by cell phone. They acted pissed off but in a week it was legend. I made them read "A Good Man Is Hard to Find." Next I made them read "A Good Man Is Hard to Find." Then I made them read "A Good Man Is Hard to Find." That's all we did. We read "A Good Man Is hard to Find" over and over.

Because long ago in a galaxy far, far away, I awoke one morning and made love to Diosa. Leni Riefenstahl had died, but we made love anyway. Everyone in the house was on a new diet. Everyone in the house could eat only protein or fresh fruits and vegetables. Like in *Sleeper*, hot fudge sundaes were now good for us. Everyone now knew that carbohydrates were bad. Diosa pulled down my fat pants. There, sitting right in the middle of me, was a gigantic hard-on, even bigger than usual.

"Must be the protein diet," Diosa said. "Think it will fit?"

"Yes," I said optimistically. Boy, did I feel good. I liked nothing better than having a big fat hard-on that was going to be inside Diosa. Diet aside, Diosa had lately taken up swimming and under the inextinguishable layers of her softness, I felt the ripple of new muscle, or old muscle aroused to newness, this, and her defiant eyes softening to yes, her yes rising, her hair layered in blonde woven in black and red and green falling on her shoulders, this and the quiet fact that everyone knew, everyone knew and quietly kept quiet beyond reason, a silence that only confirmed that she was the most beautiful woman in the world and with her love she'd killed a hundred men, with a mind, if one were to believe in mind, as clever and lethal as sunlight on a fern, as lethal as her love; I went to her heat with my lips but she grabbed me by the hair and pulled me up; she grabbed my dick in her miracle clutch; it seemed, or she made it seem, that I was too big for her hand to fit around; and though she was hot and wet, she could barely fit me in; and then that slow exhilaration of our rocking, inch by inch, I slowly entered; she clutched at my shoulders, I rose up, angling against her G-spot and she clutched and shuddered; her teeth clenched; we rose from the bed, into the air; we floated; we stared into each other past each other's eyes into some infinity; and then I suddenly felt like I was going to pass out.

I clung to Diosa, my hot sweat turning cold. I plunged deeper, looking for a place where she wouldn't rock me as violently, but fold around me, hold me, massage me, but she harder rocked into me harder. It was glorious, but my heart fluttered and I started to dream. Maybe I would die. Maybe I'd die while making love and this time I'd be dead for good. Or I could come, but I didn't want to come this soon and I didn't want to die before I came. I remembered, years ago, after a morning making love to Diosa, I'd run in the mountains and then, while picking up Jesus from school, I'd passed out on the playground. Lying there, immobile, I watched the paramedics move over me. I waved to the crowd of children as the firemen packed me into the back of the ambulance, my first ambulance ride! "I had an ACCIDENT!" I wanted to shout, just like in "A Good Man Is Hard to Find." "I had an ACCIDENT!" As the medics came into focus around me, I said, "What happened?" and someone answered, "We're checking you for a heart attack. What did you do today? Did you do anything unusual?" "Made love," I said. "Ran in the mountains." "Did you eat?" "No," I said. "Not yet." "How hard did you make love?" "Hard," I said. The men nodded. They rolled me from the ambulance and slammed me into the hospital and hooked me up to machines. Nurses ran in and out. In and out. Then in, then out, and then stopped. I watched my blood pressure, 110 over 60, my heart beat at around 62. In a while a curly haired nurse walked in. "Guess I'm not having a heart attack," I said. She felt my head, my wrist, then left me there with my machines. Bleep. Bleep. Whirrr. Bleep. An hour. Two. Then Diosa came striding through the emergency room, heads turning to her and following like radar dishes. She came into the cardio room and stood over me.

"You're all right," she said.

"Look at my machines," I said.

She did. "You had to tell them we made love."

"They asked," I said.

"And you told them," said Diosa.

"You kill with your cunt," I said.

Outside the glass walled cardio room a crowd had gathered. I pointed. Diosa turned. I felt like I was being watched by the album cover of Sergeant Pepper's Lonely Hearts Club Band. Now, deep inside Diosa and on the edge of nothingness, I was glad for the memory. It was much better than reciting the standings of all the Major League Baseball Divisions, National and American. After I came, I stayed hard and Diosa worked me for what I was worth as we floated down to the bed; when I softened I withdrew and went down on her.

"No," she said. "No. Enough."

A good sign. Heap good sign. I rolled away. Looked at her. She knew.

"I thought I had you that time," she said.

As she showered I staggered to the living room for coffee and there, on the front page, this:

Obituaries
September 10, 2003
EDWARD TELLER: 1908-2003
Force Behind H-Bomb, 'Star Wars'

I looked up to find Diosa in front of me, hair wound in a towel, her skin flush, softness pouring from the terry wrap that pushed up her breasts and fell like a dress above her knees. For a moment my head swam again.

"There are never any women in the *LA Times* Obituaries," she said.

"Leni Riefenstahl," I said.

"Section B," Diosa said. "Teller got front page. Besides," she said, turning away, rubbing the towel that stacked her hair and then letting the wet hair fall on her shoulders, "besides, she's not from here. Check the Obituaries. Only men die in Los Angeles."

I rustled through the local section of the *Times*. Found the deaths. A judge, a surgeon, several corporate moguls. All men.

"Only the men are dying," said Diosa.

"You don't have anything to do with this?" I said.

"I don't think so." She walked away, the backs of her calves like slender urns.

In the coming days I began to check the obituaries even before I opened the Sports Page. Only men. Even in the sports section, under Miscellany, where at the end of the column they listed "Passings." Men only. What did this mean? What could it mean?

I've been following the obituaries in the *LA Times* ever since. Check it out. Only men die in Los Angeles. Comedian-singer Carla Zilbersmith died in May, 2010, but she died in Berkeley. Dorothy "Dottie" Kamensheck from the All-American Girls Professional Baseball League made the paper, but she died in Palm Desert. Women don't die here. But keep it to yourself.

The Immense Jolt of Loving

For you the simulations of my mental instability become
untranslatable. For you in the face of the air that separates us
I purchase a revolver. I spit, I shut, I kick the curtains, the
bolts, the forest of doors. You are sexual copper. You
lie like a rose on our bed of poetic manifestations. Do you
find me charming or idiotic? All this lavishness. Too much
biting in the middle of the night? I've put the photographic
plate of my face into an acid bath. You'll be shocked by
what emerges, more or less. The bones of one continuous
escape.

—Diosa

Are You Awake My Darling

Are you awake my darling in this horrible room with its dance of walls and ghosts, a map of crucifix, a Virgin Larry, your somber pulse upon my ear, in your chest that listless thumping? At you I wave the flag of simplicity. At you I bare simplicity too soft to understand. Who is that phantom shuffling behind you? What is he doing? A soft shoe? Making it snow webs and dreams. I touch your hair. I touch your hair. I want to find one small place inside me where you have never been.

—Shark

EAST OF HOLLYWOOD

IT ALL STARTED OUT innocently enough, but it turned into an extravaganza! I published a book about the Beats. I'd read all of Jack Kerouac and seven biographies about him. I don't know how that happened. It was an accident. I'd read a bunch of Ginsberg and Burroughs, so I read their biographies. I read Snyder. I read Corso. I read Ferlinghetti, and John Clellan Holmes's *Go*! I read Jan Kerouac. I read Neal Cassady's *The First Third*. Hell, I even read Joyce Johnson. So I wrote a book about Jack Kerouac coming back from the dead, traveling around the U.S. and running into the other Beats. I called it *Off the Road*. *Off the Road* by Shark Rosenthal. I thought it was pretty darn funny. Every time I finished a section I mailed it off to the Beat it was about and asked for a comment. Burroughs ignored me, as did Corso and Carolyn Cassady. Ginsberg's secretary, Bob Rosenthal, sent me a post card wishing me luck. Ferlinghetti sent me an unsigned rejection notice. Up in Davis, CA, I handed the book to Gary Snyder personally. He was really little. Snyder giggled and handed it back. "Thank you," said Gary Snyder. So I made up the commentary after every chapter except for Ferlinghetti's rejection notice. For the back of the book I made up blurbs from the dead Beatniks: Holmes, Neal Cassady, Rexroth; lucky for me Burroughs died just in time and gave me a nasty blurb. I also took a blurb from my then neighbor, the iron sculptor Norm Grochowski. Norm was in AA and used to sneak over to my place to drink tequila. Of course he'd wait till I wasn't there. He found the galleys on my bar table and read them. "Is this true?" said Norm. "I can't believe it's true." "It's all true," I said and blurbed him.

It took a while but I finally published that book with Les Rocks Press run by Randall Dodge who happened to be tied for the second smartest man on the planet (who was he tied with?). Back then Dodge worked in a cubicle in the giant MGM building in Santa Monica (now he works for Disney) where he played watchdog over credit fraud, not money credit but movie credits. You wouldn't believe the legal battles over how big the names are printed and where they appear, the backstabbing, the bribes. Anyway, Randall ran Les Rocks Press on MGM hardware. Billed his software purchases to MGM. Wiled away his dead MGM hours setting pages, editing and copyediting. MGM hired book cover art designers, printed Les Rocks stationery, hired a PR man named Samson Agonistes who was really Randall Dodge himself, paid for on-demand printing, advertised in *Poets and Writers* and the *AWP Chronicle*, financed a Les Rocks website. For no intent but all purposes my Beatnik book was the first book published by MGM.

"I want an ad in *The New York Review of Books*," I said.

"Shark, don't get greedy," said Dodge.

"How about a review in the *New York Times?*"

"We can't afford the bribe."

"The *LA Times?*"

"They're even more expensive."

"You're MGM!" I said.

"We are not MGM," said Dodge. "We have to lie low."

"How low?"

"Pretty darn low," Dodge said. "I still want to publish Samson Agonistes's book of poems."

Whatever the reasons, my novel *Off the Road* became the first book ever published about Jack Kerouac and the Beats that never made it into City Lights Bookstore in North Beach, though I did get sued for $100,000 by Carolyn Cassady who hadn't read my novel but had just published her own book entitled *Off the Road* and figured I must have at least stolen something. "It's all stolen," I wrote her lawyer. "Every word is a word Kerouac once used. They're just out of order." Anyway, I changed the title to *Avatar Angel*.

I found Carolyn Cassady's book in City Lights on the walls of shelving dedicated to the Beats and everything that had ever been written by them or about them except for my book. I went over to the check out counter and handed *Avatar Angel* to the clerk, a young, intellectual Asian in a plaid shirt and glasses. The kid had Berkeley written all over him.

"Have you seen this book?" I said.

"No," said the clerk.

"Would you like to?"

"No," the young man said.

"Why not?" I said.

"No one has ever asked for it," said the clerk.

I spread my arms, bookstore wide. "People asked for all these books?" I said.

The clerk lowered his eyelids. I went to the suggestion box and made one hundred and one requests for my book. To no effect. Maybe it was my equivocal literary status as an Angelino, lingering between the realms of Hollywood and syntax, or my Los Angeles *duende* that made it so difficult for me to penetrate the cornices of the literary north, fly in their universe of discourse, drive in the communication highway of the Bayaria, swim the sea of Berkeley Byzantium. I was neither brie nor cheese.

"You're from LA," said the clerk. "Have a bookstore in LA sell it."

"Would I premier a movie in San Francisco?" I said to him. "We don't even have bookstores."

I looked deep into my soul. What's wrong with me? I asked. Where do I start? my soul said. That's when I stopped my soul searching.

"What is it about me?" I said to Diosa, and Randall Dodge over drinks.

"I thought the Kerouac thing would do it for us," Dodge said.

"It's not you they don't like," said Diosa. "It's your writing."

So I wrote about an eco-feminist dragon, modeled the plot after the original *Frankenstein*.

"Want another book?" I said to Dodge.

"Maybe not," said Dodge.

"Want the dragon book or my memoir?"

"They're not the same thing?"

"They're the same thing," Diosa said.

"I'm already having second thoughts," said Dodge. "Why don't you try New York?"

"That graveyard?" I said. "I want Hollywood!"

"We're Les Rocks, not Hollywood."

"You're MGM!" I said.

"What else have you got?"

"*The Heart of Darkness* on Mars? Only with Phillip Marlowe instead. I send him down the *Valles Maraneris.*"

"Want to see some surrealist poetry?" Diosa said.

"I think I do," said Randall Dodge.

"Okay," I said. "I've had it. I'm done with literary writing. Get Bill Gass on the phone."

"Who are you talking to?" said Diosa.

"No one. It's Hollywood lingo," I said. "A kind of verbal double metaphor."

"You're done with literary writing so you want to talk to William Gass?" Dodge said.

"Bill Gass."

"William Gass *The Tunnel?* William Gass *In the Heart of the Heart of the Country?*"

You have to start somewhere. It's what happens when you push a mind like mine over the edge.

"How's Mars?" Gass asked me when he picked up.

"I'm bored with Mars," I said.

"Too much sand will do that to you," said Gass.

"Maybe I'll go back to Europa."

"Never go back to Europa," said Bill Gass. "It's always a mistake to go back to Europa. Come see my Models of the Universe Museum."

"Do you want to be published by MGM?" I asked him.

"I think I'll stick with Dalkey Archive," he said. "I'd rather be unread with an unknown publisher."

"MGM is a pretty unknown publisher," I said. "Want to be in my movie?" I told him about Miko Shay and Marco Polo, the two young guys who wanted to make a movie about me.

"I'll have to get permission from Mary," said Gass. He left, came back. "Mary Googled them, they aren't anywhere," he said.

"Is that a yes?"

"No."

"John Sloss is involved."

"The Sundance Sloss? *Little Miss Sunshine* Sloss?"

"Yes," I said.

"Okay," said Bill Gass. "I think Mary will go for that."

"Better call Johnny," I said to Diosa when I got off the phone. "I got him involved in my movie."

"Johnny won't have anything to do with your movie."

Diosa and Sloss were friends in high school outside Detroit. Used to get stoned with Madonna, on and on. It's all connected, you know. Every time he dropped by our place during the American Film Market he'd catch me naked in the hot tub. That's independent filmmaking, it's all timing. He was always envying our artsy road taken and promising Diosa he'd do anything he could for her.

"He always says he'll do anything he can for you."

"That's only because he can't do anything for me," said Diosa.

"But now he can help me!"

"With a movie about you that hasn't been made yet."

"It's practically a done deal," I said.

I called Sloss immediately. "Johnny, want to get behind a movie about me?" I said to him.

"How did you get this number?" said John Sloss.

"William Gass is on board."

"Who's William Gass?"

"He's a friend of your buddy Tom Wolf."

"I'm not friends with Tom Wolf," said Sloss.

"But you like him. I can get Dylan."

"Dylan Thomas? He's dead."

"Bob Dylan. My guy at MGM boxes at Dylan's gym." That was true.

"Who do you know at MGM?"

"Randall Dodge."

"MGM is going under and now I can see why," said John Sloss.

"I'll let you use my hot tub when you're in town," I told him.

"I've been in your hot tub. I'll pass."

"Johnny, just let me say you're on board," I said.

"No," said Sloss.

"I've got Johnny," I said to Diosa when I got off.

"He's never going to speak to me again," said Diosa.

Now it was back to Dodge.

"I have Gass and Sloss," I said to him.

"Gass n' Sloss?"

"How well do you know Bob Dylan?"

"No one's allowed to look at him or you're thrown out of the gym."

"Just get me in and let me get thrown out. We can shoot it on your i-phone."

"I can't get you in."

"I'm using your name," I said to him.

"Where?"

"Everywhere."

"Don't use my name," said Randall Dodge.

"And MGM," I said.

"Don't use MGM," said Randall Dodge.

"They're already in up to their noses," I said.

So all that was left was for me to talk to Miko Shay and Marco Polo and get things rolling.

"You guys said you needed backing. I got backing."

"Who?" said Miko.

"John Sloss."

"How much money?" said Marco.

"Not money, backing."

"He'll front us?" asked Miko.

"No, he's behind us" I said. "And MGM."

"MGM is disappearing," said Marco.

"MGM will never disappear," I said. "I know a guy in the credit department."

"I work at Paramount. That doesn't mean they'll front my movie," Marco said.

"You're not in the credit department."

"Will we get MGM credit cards?" said Miko.

"Let's not go into debt making this," I said.

"Distribution," said Marco.

"I'll have him talk to somebody. This is Hollywood. We can do it!"

So that's how it began. Miko and Marco showed up at my place that weekend. Marco worked the camera, Miko asked the questions.

There's film of me in my house talking about writing.

"What do you think of Cormac McCarthy?"

"I never think about Cormac McCarthy."

"What do you think of his writing?"

"What does he think of my writing?"

"We'll have to ask him," said Marco.

"Put that on the list," said Miko.

There's me riding my horse and talking about Martians, me on the Topanga Canyon overlook called Heaven and me in my cabin office on the mountaintop above Heaven. I'm in ecstasy. I'm above ecstasy. I'm at Equator Books for my book party for *The Heart of Mars*. My performance artist daughter, Jesus, is playing the sitar with Willie Nelson's sons, Mikah and Lucas: Insects vs. Robots, Reflectacles, Folk Acid, Cosmic Country.

"This place is packed!" screams Miko.

"Think it's the free beer and music?" I say. "But we sold all the books!"

"They stole all the books!" says the owner, Phil.

We corner David Eggers at the LA Book Festival in the green room.

"Do you know Shark Rosenthal?"

"No," says Eggers.

"We had lunch," I say. "You barked a lot back then."

"It was humor," says David Eggers.

"You'd just climbed Mount Kilimanjaro and did abstract paintings with elephants."

"Now I remember, Mervyn Delamore couldn't make it," says David Eggers.

"He was up north working with the Ewoks," I say.

"I think that's Miwoks," says Miko.

"Have you ever been to Jerry Brown's underground palace?" Eggers says.

I turn to the camera. "Every time I see him he asks me that," I say.

"More famous people!" said Miko.

"Then we have to go to St. Louis and Pittsburgh," I said.

"St. Louis and Pittsburgh?"

So then there's St. Louis and William Gass meeting me at the front door of his giant house.

"Long time no see," says Bill Gass. "Written anything good yet?"

Though in fact we had to shoot that scene eight times. It's a movie thing. You only *think* that documentaries are real.

There's Bill Gass and me walking down the street talking about the mansions of University City. You can buy them for a song but you can't afford to heat them.

Then there's Bill Gass pretending to read *The Heart of Mars*.

"Boy, that's embarrassing," I said to Miko.

"For who?" said Bill Gass.

Cut to dinner with Bill and Mary and me telling Mary about racing a Yak named Derek Jeter to the Chinese border.

"I don't believe a word of that," says Mary Gass.

"It's Magic Journalism," I say. "It's not about the facts."

"Could you believe it for the movie?" says Miko.

"Isn't this the movie?" says Mary.

"What's the name of this movie anyways?" says Bill.

"*The Death of Writing in America*," says Miko. "Do you think writing is dead in America?"

"Writing's not dead, publishing is dead," says Bill Gass.

The camera turns to me and I point at Bill. "He said that, I didn't," I say.

"Is it true you don't believe in meaning?" Miko asks Bill Gass.

"It depends on what you mean," Bill says.

"Did that mean anything?"

"Yes," says Mary.

"No," says Bill. "Or maybe."

"I finally found you on the internet," Mary says to Miko. "You did a documentary on the space program."

"The Jupiter probe," Miko says.

"Did you find the Shark on Europa?" says Bill.

"There are sharks on Europa?"

Gass points to me. "It's in his book."

"That was great!" yells Marco.

"Cut!" yells Miko.

"Those weren't sharks," I say. "They were Orcas."

"I thought Orcas were sharks," says Bill Gass.

"Could you say that again with the camera running?" Miko says.

On the plane to Pittsburgh, my director Miko Shay swooned. "My God, I met William Gass. I was in William Gass's house. William Gass. William Gass!"

"Calm down," I said.

"Do you know Barth, too?" said Marco.

"We talk about the difference between Pacific Ocean and Chesapeake Bay dolphins."

"Coover?"

"Our computers generate our conversations. We don't really talk."

"Chabon?"

"Like the back of my hand."

"And Bill Kittredge really told you to stop writing?"

"Only fiction."

"Did you really sleep with Pam Houston?"

"In my cowboy phase."

"You're still in a cowboy phase."

"We were both very very sleepy," I said.

And then we're in Pittsburgh where Diosa flies in to meet us at Chuck Kinder's giant house in Squirrel Hill, camera running.

"Who are these little twerps?" says Chuck Kinder.

"Where's John Sloss?" says Diane Cecily, his wife.

"Is it true Kittredge isn't speaking to you?" asks Miko.

"Just jump right in," says Kinder.

"Where did Chabon stay?"

"He didn't stay, he left," says Diane.

"Did he see the ghost?"

"Where'd you hear about the ghost?" says Kinder.

Miko points to me. "He wrote about it in the *Santa Monica Review*."

"Well you can't believe anything you read in the *Santa Monica Review*," Kinder says. He points to Diosa. "She's why Missy wears cowgirl boots in the book."

"What book?"

"*The Wonderboys*," I say.

"I only saw the movie," says Miko.

"Well she wore them in the movie, too," says Diane.

"I want *Vallejo* tattooed on my forearm," says Diosa.

"Then every girl in Pittsburgh will have Vallejo tattooed on her forearm," says Kinder.

"Cowgirl poetry," says Diosa.

"You write cowgirl poetry?" says Miko.

"Wrote, back then, in a manner of speaking."

"She started a cowgirl cult in Pittsburgh," says Kinder. "Cowgirl boots everywhere."

"Shark wrote the screenplay," says Diosa.

"Of a book of poems?"

"Finally we're talking about me," I say. "I thought this was my movie."

"Plot points," says Diosa.

"Swimming pools," I say, "movie stars."

"Sundance finalist," says Diosa.

"No shit," says Miko. He turns to Kinder. "What about Ray Carver?" he asks.

"He was Diane's boyfriend, but I stole her from him. Stole her from my best friend."

"Old story," Diane says.

"Old as the hills," says Kinder.

"Who knew Ray was a great writer?" says Diane.

"I did," says Kinder.

"It's all in *The Honeymooners*," I say. "Kittredge is in there, too."

"He stopped talking to me because he didn't like his portrayal," says Chuck.

"As a drunk," says Diane. "Too true."

"Just fun," says Kinder. "Now he's dead."

"That'll quiet you down," says Diosa.

"Carver," says Miko.

"Ray was the greatest writer who ever lived. What's more to say?"

"You're better," I say.

"You're better than me," says Chuck Kinder.

"Diosa's better than me," I say.

"Boy, I'm glad I'm not a writer," says Diane.

"Can we get drunk now?" Kinder says.

Then we have a big party. My sister, Aubrey, who lives in Pittsburgh, shows up in a skin-tight gold satin jump suit, auburn hair pouring everywhere. "Oh, don't film me, I have nothing to say," says Aubrey and proceeds to dominate the camera for an hour. Then it's off to Erie, PA, my home town. Does that sound depressing? It is.

Back in Topanga there's me opening my mail box.

"Look," I say, "Grammy tickets. Must be for my spoken word nomination."

"You have a CD?" Miko says.

Quick cut to me holding up a copy of VERB Audio Magazine.

Flip to a video of Daren Wang, publisher of VERB in Atlanta, now defunct. "The Shark is the funniest writer in America," Daren Wang says.

"Why doesn't everybody know that?" says Miko.

"Who knows anything?" says Daren Wang.

So Marco got press passes for the Grammy Awards from Paramount. "Let's go to the Grammy's!" said Miko Shay.

And it's Diosa and me at the Lifetime Achievement Awards with Leonard Cohen. Cohen thanks the Grammy's for their modest response to his work over the years. He recites "Tower of Song" and walks off the stage.

"I hitch-hiked from Detroit to Quebec when I was fifteen," Diosa tells Cohen. "I followed you around for a week."

"Do you know how many women tell me that?" Cohen says.

"Are they all from Detroit?" Diosa says.

"Or Berlin," says Cohen.

Two men point at me and make a fist. I point at them and make a fist.

At the reception we drink vodka martinis (they don't have gin). We're sitting with blues man David "Honeyboy" Edwards and his family listening to the Los Angeles All Star High School Big Jazz Band. They're pretty good. Honeyboy, a gentle, sweet guy, sits in his wheel chair and nods to the jazz.

Two more guys give me index fingers and fists. "Dude, you are so cool," says one of them.

"Thank you," I say.

"How come nobody knew you at the LA Book Festival but people know you here?" asks Miko.

"Because there I'm only pale words on pale paper, my self barely visible. Here I am visage and voice."

"They think he's somebody else," says Diosa.

"Don't put that in the movie," I say.

"Looking forward to tomorrow?" Miko asks me.

"No," I say. "I hate the Grammy's." I pull out a pocket copy of André Breton's *Arcatum 17*. "But I'm ready."

"That's not even his book. It's my book," says Diosa.

Cut to the Grammy entrance, Staples Center, Diosa, Jesus, and me on the red carpet between the filled grandstands.

"Lady Gaga! Lady Gaga!" a man shouts at Jesus. Jesus is a dead out fashion blonde. People take her picture all over LA thinking she's Lady Gaga. Lots of people start yelling at her, "Lady Gaga! Lady Gaga!" and reaching for her. Others are yelling, "Jesus! Jesus!" Jesus puts out her hands and touches them. As Jesus she has her own Club following as a performance artist at Highways, the Cozy Castle, the Viper Room, the Venice Beach Freak Show, all over: sitar playing mermaid, robot striptease, pole dancing on a crucifix, aerobics with pythons, though she looks a lot more like Lady Gaga than she does Jesus.

We have to get there early and go to the Convention Center because they only give out a dozen awards during the Grammy show, the other fifty thousand Grammy Awards are given here, in the pre-show, Best Four-Person Ensemble Doing European Circus Themes, stuff like that. Nobody goes except the people who are nominated, though they try to lure a crowd with free wine and sandwiches. After that you don't get dick. I get another index finger and fist bump. "Hope you win." "Thank you," I say.

But I don't win. Barak Obama or Jimmy Carter or somebody wins. I don't even get mentioned.

"How come they didn't read your name?" says Miko.

"They only read the top five. I probably finished sixth," I tell the camera.

We all go over to the Staples Center amidst more cheers for Lady Gaga and Jesus. We buy hot dogs, Cokes, and nachos for three hundred dollars and eat them behind an AT&T advertisement to get out of the limelight. Then we go to our seats and wait for a million years, but finally the show starts. There I am reading *Arcatum 17* while Lady Gaga and Elton John perform. A little guy in glasses, thin hair, comes up and hands me a Grammy Awards program.

"Would you three sign this?"

"Sure," I say. "Who am I?"

"I thought she was Lady Gaga," says the guy, "but now I guess maybe not."

"She's Jesus," I say.

"That'll do." He points at me. "Jeff Bridges."

"Now I get it," says Diosa.

"Sissy Spacek?" he says to Diosa.

"She's only four feet tall," Diosa says.

"Loretta Lynn?"

"Could be my grandmother, Jesus."

"Yes?" says Jesus.

"Wow. Jeff Bridges reading André Breton at the Grammy's," the guy says.

Then the cavalry comes, or the opposite of the cavalry, Diosa's brother, Barely, Grammy Awards Vice President. Diosa introduces him to everybody.

"Having a good time?" says Barely.

"I have an obstructed view," I say.

"Isn't this a conflict of interests?" says Miko.

"Grammy tickets?" says Barely.

"Holy shit!" I say. "Where'd that little guy go? He lifted my André Breton!"

"Surreal," Diosa says.

Thousands of hours of filming later Miko and Marco were ready to wrap things up. "We need closure!" said Miko Shay.

"There's no closure in life, Miko," I said.

"This isn't life!" said Marco. "This is Hollywood!"

"Stop getting excited!" I said.

"Who did this book cover?" said Miko. He held up a galley of my next book about my trip to the Himalayas. "It's terrific."

"Gronk."

"Gronk! *Brain Flame* Gronk? Let's go film Gronk!"

"That will give us closure?"

"Just watch," said Miko, whatever that meant.

We headed for Gronk's downtown loft on Seventh and Spring but we got cut off at the pass. Somebody was making a movie! We had to park on 10th and Grand. But when we got to Spring Street motorcycle police closed off the street. Guys in t-shirts and tank shirts and AK-47's, more guys in suits with hand guns stopped us, holding up badges.

"You can't go in, we're making a movie," said a thug in a wife-beater.

"We're making a movie," I said.

"No, we're making a movie," said the thug.

"Is that real?" said Diosa. She pointed to his weapon.

"Everything is real," he said.

"Real what?" I said.

"A real movie."

"The lines are getting fuzzy," said Miko.

"Put that camera down," the thug said to Marco.

Just then a loudspeaker blared out. "Everybody get off the street! Everybody off the street! We're about to start the rain!"

"You're going to get wet," said the thug. "Real wet."

And then the water began to pour from above. High above us, at the top of the warehouses, hung lines of pipes that began to spew water onto Spring Street. A downpour! A block of downtown Los Angeles inundated with black rain.

"Let's make a break for it!" yelled Diosa and headed down Spring.

I followed. The camera followed. Shots rang out. We ducked into Gronk's entryway and hid behind some pillars. The rain came down. We had to call a friend of Gronk's who called Gronk to let us in. That's how famous he is. But he comes down and greets us in the foyer, Gronk paintings in twisted profusion all over the walls.

"Oh my," says Gronk. "The rain machine again."

"I'm all greasy," I say.

"They put oil in the water to make the street shine under the lights," says Gronk. "It looks more real."

"Where are they setting this movie?" says Diosa. "Do you know?"

"New York, of course," says Gronk.

Gronk's building is labyrinthine. We take an elevator up two floors, enter a hallway, take a right, a left, another left, go up a short stairway and down a short stairway, take a right, step onto a platform, step off the platform; everywhere there are paintings, paintings, paintings, twisting sculptures of vaguely human figures, huge glass brains, and now the long hallways are covered with murals, intricate, vague figurations of plants, animals, people, penises, lots of penises, color color color, down another long hallway of the same, then to the right, a patio covered with the beginnings of wooden things like unfinished shacks and scaffolding covered by cacti and succulents, and then a doorway opening into a dark cavernous loft filled with more painting and sculpture (I've been here dozens of times and every time I get lost), tables are covered with prints and glass brains, some chairs, a bar, a big piano almost unnoticeable amidst the dark and art, a bookcase full of B sci-fi and monster movies (an addiction shared by me, and William Gass, too; Gass prefers *Godzilla*; Gronk, *Gamura* and *The Giant Claw*; I lean toward *Gorgo* and *Mothra*); there are some futons surrounding a giant, really giant TV screen. We're standing at the bar. I open a bottle of wine.

Gronk looks at the camera, then at me. "So you're making a movie," he says.

"It's not as good as *The Giant Claw*," I say.

"The special effects are better," says Diosa.

"I'm writing a book," says Gronk.

"Does it have words?" I say.

"Not really. I'm inventing a picture alphabet, but every letter is new."

"Talk about denying closure," I say to Miko.

There's a roar from outside and the building shakes a little.

"I guess they blew something up," says Gronk.

"What's the name of your book?" asks Miko.

"*A Giant Claw*," says Gronk. "What's the name of your movie?"

"*The Death of Writing in America*," I say.

"I like that," says Gronk. "Do you kill anybody?"

"Everybody."

"Even the monster?"

"The monster comes back," I say. "But there's nobody left. Everybody's dead."

"You'll need another monster for a fight," says Gronk. "I could be a monster."

"You are already the monster," says Diosa.

"I like being a monster," says Gronk.

Anyway, it goes on like that for a long time, that's why you have editing. We finish another bottle of wine.

"Going to get your closure?" I say to Miko.

"If I have to do it with my bare hands," he says.

"That's the spirit," I say.

"Think Sloss will go for it?"

"It's right up his alley," I say. "Or down his alley. One of those."

"MGM folded," says Marco.

"Dodge is with Disney now. We'll be fine," I tell them.

We finish up and Gronk walks us out through the dark maze of murals and art, but outside the foyer it's still raining like hell. Water is flowing up over the curb.

"We better go up a floor," says Gronk. "Sometimes it floods."

"They can't just turn it off?" says Marco.

"Sometimes it just gets out of hand," says Gronk.

From the roof it looks like things are out of hand. The water rises six feet, eight feet, ten; it glistens black under the light that pours from windows and street lamps.

"How is this possible?" says Marco.

"How long does this last?" asks Miko.

"Forty days? Forty nights?" says Gronk.

"Then we send out the doves," I say.

"Let's call out for Chinese," says Diosa.

"They can deliver?" says Miko.

"They have a junk," Gronk says.

"What's that?" screams Marco. He points to a huge object swelling from the black depths and skimming just beneath the surface. A reptilian head the size of a Toyota emerges, blinks, submerges.

"Just the giant turtle," says Gronk. "He comes out when it floods."

"We're trapped here?" says Miko.

"My God," whispers Marco. His face is a visage of stunned enigma. "Trapped inside a Hollywood movie."

"Relax," says Gronk. "I'll go get my boat."

THE TEN OF WRITER

NOT LONG AFTER the Grammy Awards me and Diosa were hanging out with Diosa's brother, Barely, and his wife, the Fire Aunt Christi, at their place in Silver Lake. Their house was near the top of a walk street of all stairs. Hundreds of steps. Hundreds of stairs. The Fire Aunt was a yoga teacher. On top of the yoga, the stairs solved the whole aerobics thing. But going up those stairs Diosa had to take a lot of breaks and smoke a lot of cigarettes.

Barely had been an actor and director at the Source Theatre back in D.C. before he took a job running Theater LA, a theatre consortium in downtown Los Angeles.

"We want to kick this up a notch," the board told him.

"Okay!" said Barely.

"No more sit-com showcases for TV actors."

"Real theatre," said Barely.

"That's right," they said. "And make lots of money!"

"You want to make lots of money doing real theatre?" said Barely.

It was downhill from there. A year later he got deposed. A theatre *coup d'etat*. Out with Pinter. In with *Paint Your Wagons*. Barely took a job running a community theatre out in Riverside, but the commute was killing him. *Brigadoon* was killing him. He was like totally *Les Miserables*.

"What should I do?" Barely asked me one night over bourbon on the rocks.

"Run off and join the circus?" I said.

And he did. This is why you don't give people advice. But you know, I teach for a living. I'm not used to anybody paying attention. Barely ran away and joined the Big Apple Circus. Then he became the mayor of the Big Apple Circus. Started hanging out with Sean Lennon and Whoopi Goldberg, Woody Allen, those types. When he was done with that he was unemployed for two years and began experimenting with legal hallucinogens that he got over the Internet. Went on a drug safari down the Amazon in Peru where he ran into a boatload of Grammy trustees coming from the other direction. Nobody found God but the Grammy Awards found a new vice president. As Barely said, "Go figure."

Grammy VP though he was, since his circus days what he really wanted to do was run his own circus. He wanted his circus to be based on the Tarot. He'd just spent too much time getting drunk with gypsies is how I saw it. His plan was that every night, before the show, he'd come out in his top hat and tails and do a Tarot reading of the audience, center tent, with giant Tarot Cards ten feet tall. The following circus would be based on the reading, like a spontaneous Tarot *Cirque du Soleil*. All he needed was sixty million dollars to get started.

"Sounds good to me," I said. "All you need is sixty million dollars."

"Except that nobody will give you sixty million dollars to start a Tarot Card circus," said Diosa.

"But what if they did," said Barely. He was kind of dark and handsome, with a big head like an actor. "What if, say, I read Whoopi Goldberg's Tarot and she gives me sixty million dollars?"

"You've talked to Whoopi Goldberg?" said Diosa.

"Not yet."

"It would fail," Diosa said. "You'd be sixty million in debt."

"My big sister," said Barely. "So practical. What if someone would have told you it was impractical to be a surrealist poet?"

"I didn't need sixty million dollars to be a surrealist poet."

"But what if you did?"

"There'd be fewer of them," I said.

"How many are there now?" said the Fire Aunt.

Was that a good question or what?

"Circuses are kind of surreal," said Barely

"You guys have surrealism in your blood," I said. "Why don't you just listen to voices like Jin-Jin?"

"That's New Age, I'm old school," said Barely.

"Isaiah?" I said. "Moses?"

"He talked to God. He didn't hear voices."

"Fine line," I said.

"You have to have balance, inner balance, true balance," said Fire Aunt Christi, who everyone called the Fire Aunt because of her hot temper. She was thin and blonde. "If you have balance, if you, yourself, have balance, then everything will balance out around you. Everything will work out."

"See," said Barely.

"Does that count for the worse," Diosa said.

"I joined the circus and things worked out. Took a drug safari and look what happened."

"You don't believe in the Tarot," I said to Barely.

"What's to believe?" Barely said. "It's you and the cards. There's you. There's the cards. Why you? Why these cards? Why not other cards? But no, it's these cards. These cards now. Next time different cards. Different you."

"You sure make the arbitrary sound arbitrary," I said.

"Let me read your Tarot, Shark," Barely said to me.

"No," I said.

"Just pick a card then," said Barely.

"No."

"Come on, Shark," said the Fire Aunt. "Do it for me."

"Yeah," said Barely, "do it for the Fire Aunt."

"Or I'll get mad," said the Fire Aunt.

One thing I didn't want was the Fire Aunt falling out of balance. "Okay," I said. "I'll pick a card. But you're all going to regret this."

Barely spread the deck like a fan in front of me, face down. "Pick a card," said Barely.

"Any card," I said.

I looked at the deck. I knew this was a big mistake. Something wonderful or horrible would have to happen and then, inevitably, it would arbitrarily happen, eventually. Who needs the cards?

"Go ahead, Shark," said Diosa.

"Come on, Shark," said the Fire Aunt, "go ahead."

So I picked a card. I turned it over. It was a man lying on his back with ten swords in his chest.

"Whoa!" said Barely.

"Macabre," I said.

"You don't know what macabre means," said Diosa.

"It's a lot of swords," I said.

"In your chest," said Diosa.

"My chest?" I said.

"You should have gone with your initial instinct," said the Fire Aunt. "And not done this."

"What is it?" I said.

"You don't want to know," said the Fire Aunt.

"I can just make it up as I go along?" I said.

"Maybe we should try another card," said Barely.

"No more cards," I said.

"I'm afraid I have to agree with the Shark on that one," said the Fire Aunt.

"What's the card?" I said. I turned to Diosa. "Do you know what it is?"

"It's the ten of Swords," said Barely.

"It's the Ten of Writer," Diosa said.

TRADER JOE'S,
A PARABLE, A PROPHESY

THERE ARE TWO REASONS to live in Los Angeles: the weather and
Trader Joe's. Entertainment, food, the ocean and mountains, you can
find those other places. You might say, well, they've got a Trader Joe's in
Manhattan now. Right. One. And it doesn't sell booze. And at the Joe's you
can get it for half what you pay anywhere else. That goes for gourmet and
natural foods, too, but that you might know, even in New York.

My Joes' is in the Valley. I parked my truck, got my shopping cart from
the cart dump off in the parking lot, and entered. I put some Canadian
smoked salmon in my basket. I found hard pretzels baked by Snyder's of
Hanover (not to be confused with Snyder of Berlin) (how many people
actually confused Snyder's of Hanover with Snyder of Berlin?) and I put
the box of pretzels in my basket. I collected a bottle of calcium, magnesium
and zinc tablets and a bottle of saw palmetto oil capsules. I picked up a liter
of Monopolowa potato vodka, nine bucks a liter, and put it in my basket.
Picked up some California, French, Spanish, and Argentinean wine for about
six dollars a bottle. Bought cheese, bread, food, then got in line to check out.

Now comes a universal law. The whole world is just like the post office,
even the Trader Joe's. Everybody is in a hurry when they're waiting in line,
but when they finally reach the front of the line they are no longer in a hurry.
The woman in front of me was buying wine, but she had become indecisive

as to what bottles she should keep. She requested several versions of her purchase rung up and added so she could gauge some combination of what she wanted to spend and what she wanted to buy. The combinations were infinite. Could she have done this in front of the wine racks instead of in front of the cashier? Yes. In fact, there's always somebody at the wine racks to give advice.

Her big, round butt spread, her shoulders hunched, her voice squeaked. She wondered if someone could go to the shelves for her and get something different. Finally, her purchase chosen and rung up, now she decided how she might pay. Don't ever think about that ahead of time. Here, everybody lives like the fifth contestant on *The Family Feud*. They don't even think about the answer to the same question until the host asks *them*, and then they can't think of anything. Myself, I'm a man of leisure. I got nowhere to go. I pull out my copy of Bolaño's *Last Evenings on Earth*.

Other lines came and went while the woman contemplated how she should pay for her purchase. Cards shuffled in and out of her wallet. Cash was counted. Debit cards were considered, then credit cards. She decided on cash. Couldn't find the exact change. I waited. Yes, the world could end. It could end now. I'm ready to die in line at the Woodland Hills' Trader Joe's. Besides, choosing the wrong line is another universal law. We are all, always, in the wrong line.

Suddenly the Express Line emptied. A young guy with a long Mohawk said to me, "Want to come over here?"

"I'm using a debit card," I said.

"That's okay," the kid said, "there's nobody in line."

I shifted to the front on the Express Line. In an instant, a half-dozen cash-only express shoppers piled up behind me. I ran my debit card while the kid rang up my stuff. I put it in my reusable Joe's bags while he did. The kid sent my card through. It didn't work.

"Try it again," the cashier said.

I tried it again.

"Try it again," the kid said.

I tried it again.

"Try it again," the kid said.

I tried it again.

"Try it again."

"Maybe I should stop trying it again," I said.

You think they make up this kind of dialogue on Sponge Bob, but they don't.

"Let me try," said the kid. He ran my card through the machine. It failed. He ran it through again. Again and again the young cashier ran my debit card through the machine and again and again it failed as the Express Line grew dangerously long behind me.

"Run it as credit," I said.

"Let me try punching it in as debit," said the cashier.

He ran the card. The machine began to click, the cashier offered a wise smile. The machine rejected the card.

"Just punch the card number through as credit," I said.

"I'll try punching it through as a debit again," said the young Mohawked cashier.

I turned. The Express Line now stretched precipitously through the store like an Anaconda. It was a good thing Jesus wasn't there because deep in the recesses of the store arose the weeping and gnashing of teeth. I spread my arms to the crowd. "Aren't you glad you used the Express Lane?" I said.

"I always get in the wrong line," the woman behind me said. "It's the story of my life."

"It's everybody's story," I said.

The machine rejected my card again.

"I'll try punching your number through as credit now," the kid said to me.

I looked at the young cashier. "I'm sorry," I said.

"It doesn't matter," said the cashier. "Any time now we're all going to die at the same moment, so what does it matter?"

"What if we die at different moments?" I said to him.

"Same thing," he said.

To my left, a Russian family had spread out, planting themselves strategically in different lines. Somebody noticed. Yelled at them. A riot broke out. Cheese, wine, bodies on the floor.

"Won't someone think of the children?" a woman screamed.

"You think they'd want balloons?" said my cashier.

And almost immediately a manager appeared handing out balloons. He slipped on some wine or blood. Broke his hip.

"When you think of the children things always get worse," I said.

"I'm practically a child myself," said my cashier.

"People say LA is laid back," I said to him. "But it's not. We're tense and edgy. Look at the freeways. Remember the Rodney King thing? The whole town blew up."

"I don't think I was born yet," said my cashier. "But my father said that's how we got our TV."

"Do you think this will spread into the street?" I said.

"I hope so," he said, "it's getting dangerous in here. Hey, your card went through."

In the parking lot the sun was setting and a full moon, as red as a Trader Joe's sign, was on the rise. Ambulances and paramedic trucks screamed in, dogs howled. Then the short, balding types with Apple laptops appeared from behind the hedges and around the corner of the building, even before the news trucks. Their computers dripped quicksilver. They spouted fangs. They wanted stories. They wanted blood.

AT THE UNIVERSITY
OF LA-LA HOLY

"HELLO, PROFESSOR SHARK?" said a voice on my phone. "My name is Rhonda Riordon and you are the Faculty Advisor for English Majors whose names begin with R or S and my last name begins with R so you are my Advisor?"

"Your logic is impeccable," I said.

"Logic?" said Rhonda Riordon.

"Have you thought anymore about majoring in philosophy?" I suggested sagaciously.

"Would that require any reading?" said Rhonda Riordon.

"No," I said. "None."

"I don't like reading. That's why I'm an English Major."

"So you're a writer," I said.

"I'm Writing Emphasis," Rhonda Riordon said. "But I don't like writing so much either, I find. I like thinking sometimes."

"Philosophy for you," I said.

"Don't you think it's unfair that Spanish speaking students get to major in Spanish?" said Rhonda Riordon.

"How about Theology? You believe in God, don't you?"

"Is that all you have to do?"

"I think so," I said. "If you do a Buddhism emphasis you don't even have to do that."

"The English Major should be more like the Spanish Major," Rhonda Riordon said.

"Everyone should just be able to major in speaking their own language and get a degree," I said. "I'm for that, as long as they can use a cell phone."

"I'm using one right now!" said Rhonda Riordon.

"Exactly," I said. "Listen, Rhonda Riordon," I foolishly said into the phone, "is there a reason you called?"

"I don't mean to be pushy, Professor Shark, but I'd like some advice. My last name begins with R and you are the Advisor for people whose last names begin with R or S?"

"I think philosophy is the ticket for you," I said. "Or theology. That's my advice."

"What are your office hours?" asked Rhonda Riordon.

"They are the hours I am in my office," I said.

"But what are they?" Rhonda Riordon asked.

"What would you like them to be?" I said.

"When can I see you?"

"You meant *when* are my office hours," I said. "Have you ever been to my office, Rhonda Riordon?"

"That was my next question," said Rhonda Riordon. "Once I thought I was outside your office, but there was a lot of talking inside and I was afraid to knock."

"Was my name on the door?" I said.

"There was a picture of an alligator climbing a wall," said Rhonda Riordon. "Underneath it said, 'Bill climbed the wall.'"

"Bill is the alligator's name," I said. "You can pretty much figure out everything I have to say about the world from there, so you don't need to come in."

There was a little bit of silence after that.

"Everything?" Rhonda Riordon finally said.

"Listen, Rhonda Riordon," I said, "if you come to my office hours and the door is closed and you hear voices, knock."

"I won't interrupt?"

"You will, but it means I'm by myself. If somebody's with me I leave the door open," I told her.

"I've heard this about you," said Rhonda Riordon. "That you say things nobody can understand and then you laugh."

"Did I do that?" I said. "Have I failed to be understood?"

"Oh, why are you my advisor?" cried Rhonda Riordon.

"Because your name begins with R?" I ventured.

"Did I hear laughing?" Rhonda Riordon said.

"Did I say something funny?"

"Professor Shark, let me just say that you are very enigmatic," said Rhonda Riordon.

"But was I any help?" I said.

"Well, maybe," said Rhonda Riordon, "but I don't think so."

"Why don't you come by during office hours?" I suggested. Because it wasn't that I wanted to be difficult or unhelpful, it was that I hated advising, hated advice, hated to get it, hated to give it. It made me a bad advisor. On an even more superficial level, I found that advice implicitly condoned several specious ontic entities like free will, mind, and temporal causality in which I did not want to give the illusion that I made any investment. On the other hand, if I thought that it ever did anybody any good at all, regardless of its ineffectiveness, I'd dish it out freely. Or send them to Serum. La-La Holy should hire Serum.

Once upon a time I was so bad at advising and there were so many complaints, I was relieved of duty. Ever so briefly, during that short span, I came to believe that if you were really bad at something, somebody really might step in and prevent you from doing it. But I was wrong. One day I strolled across the hall and into the department mailroom, an idle foray into the impression that I feigned communication, and discovered that not only had my student worker failed to remove my mail from my mailbox and put it in the trash, but there, on the wall, bigger than daylight, spread a list of Faculty Advisors, and next to the majors R through S, my name had unimaginably returned.

I tore the list off the wall, but it didn't do any good. They found me. They came to me. Then I discovered that my classes had filled to the brim. How could that happen? I checked with the registrar, but nobody who showed up for my classes was actually registered for them. My registered students never attended. Sometimes nobody registered at all. In time, it occurred to me to ask for a few names. A pregnant girl named Sharon Tate. An older man, he called himself a returned student, named Bella Lugosi. I went to my chair, Blind Ray Hynde.

"I thought I'd been fired from advising," I said.

"Haven't you?" he said.

"Haven't I?"

"Back by popular demand, I bet," Blind Ray Hynde said. "Is that your phone I hear ringing?"

"Hello, Professor Shark?" said the voice on the other end. "My name is Di-di Wallport and you are the English Department Faculty Advisor R through S?"

"I am?" I said.

"I'd like some advice about my son?"

"Doesn't Wallport begin with a W?" I said.

"But son begins with an S," said Di-di Wallport.

"I don't think that's how it works," I said.

"Do I need to inform you that I'm a paying customer at your place of business, Professor Shark?" Di-di Wallport said. "My son is thinking of changing his major."

"I advise him to major in philosophy," I said.

"Do you think he'd be a good English major?"

"Does he speak English?" I said.

"I don't know," Di-di Wallport said. "It's hard to say. How long have you known him?"

"I never heard of him," I said.

"He's your advisee!" insisted Di-di Wallport.

"He's a W!" I said.

"He's my son, son with an S!" exclaimed Di-di Wallport.

A knock came on the door. "The door was shut and I heard voices," a girl said. She pushed open my office door where I sat on the phone, in front of my ancient computer, amidst my collection of second hand paperback sci-fi novels, two thousand primary source philosophy books, every word ever written by Jack Kerouac, and over four hundred rubber scale model dinosaurs. She was tall and slender, her black, black hair falling over her russet cheeks, full lips, sapphire eyes, a brooding, intelligent forehead, full breasts pouring from her scoop-necked t-shirt; yes, inevitably, I was Professor Shark, Faculty Advisor for English Majors R through S, and she was Rhonda Riordon?

HEALTH AND EDUCATION

ONE DAY Diosa got a headache. The next day she got a cough.

"You know where this is going," she said to me.

"Bronchitis," I said. "Let's go to the doctor."

"They won't do anything. I don't have a fever."

"Lie."

"They'll take my temperature."

"Let's go to Mexico and get antibiotics," I said.

"Why don't I save them?" said Diosa. "Give me a cigarette."

But we lucked out and she got a fever the next day. The doctor gave her Cipro or something like that. I drove her home. She got in the door and started to wheeze.

"What's the matter?" I said.

Diosa's eyes bugged out. "You fucking idiot," Diosa said.

"Where's your inhaler?" I said.

"How should I know?" said Diosa. She gasped. "I can't breathe."

I'd saved Jesus' life on one occasion and Diosa's on several others, all of which made her regard me with a certain suspicion. You just can't trust somebody who's saving your life all the time. It meant they were around you too much. And then you were supposed to forgive them for stuff. It made you sappy when you got drunk and thought about them.

I rummaged around in the bathroom drawers, the bedroom drawers, the kitchen drawers and came up with a gray Ventolin inhaler. I rushed back upstairs. Diosa sucked on the thing. "Empty," she gasped.

"I'll call the doctor," I said.

I got on the phone and pressed the emergency number, waited on hold until a nurse came on. "My wife can't breathe," I said. I hate the word *wife*, but sometimes you can't get around it with any alacrity.

"Is she one of our patients?" the nurse said.

"Does it matter? She can't breathe."

"Go to an emergency room."

"Doctor Data's," I said.

"Just a minute," said the nurse. She came back in about five. "Is she still breathing?"

"Barely," I said.

"Just a minute," said the nurse.

"Do you know what it's like?" said Diosa. "I'm fucking dying."

The nurse came back on the line about three minutes later. "Your wife was just here, Mr. Diosa," the nurse said.

"Shark," I said. "I'm Shark. She's Diosa."

"Well, she was just here."

"She was breathing then," I said. "She just had a fever and a cough."

"Well what do you want now?"

"She can't breathe," I said.

"Just a minute," said the nurse.

"Not to be able to breathe?" Diosa said.

"I'm on hold," I said.

"It's frightening," said Diosa.

The nurse came back on. "Yes?" she said.

"I'm Shark. My wife can't breathe."

"Just a minute," she said.

Diosa sucked on her empty inhaler. "Give me the fucking phone," she said. When the nurse came back on Diosa said, "Get the fucking doctor."

"I'm afraid she's with someone," said the nurse.

"Get the doctor before I die," said Diosa.

Eventually Dr. Data got on the phone and told Diosa that she'd have Nurse Alvara call in a prescription for Ventolin. Diosa could pick it up immediately. So I packed the wheezing Diosa back into my truck and drove back up the coast to Malibu while Diosa sat there, hand spread over her breasts, pale, pissed, glowering, silent but for the broken vacuum cleaner sound in her chest.

At the pharmacy the prescription wasn't in yet. "I'll call over there," said the clerk. She put down the phone. "They're busy, they said they'd call back."

"She can't breathe," I said.

"I'm feeling a little better," said Diosa. "Let's have lunch and come back."

"Lunch?" I said. Diosa loved lunch because it broke up the day. I hated lunch because it always came in the middle of everything. Often you had to eat it with people you didn't know or people you knew and didn't like. Then Diosa would sit in front of her BLT and pick at the bacon and me, who wasn't even hungry, guzzled a chardonnay and nervously gulped down every morsel. Then I'd have to give up supper or bourbon or just get fat.

We walked around the corner where I stopped to look at the thousand dollar kitties in the Malibu Pet Store, then we went inside the Marmalade Café. Richard Dean Anderson was at the next table, you know, McGuyver, Jack on *Stargate SG-1*. He worked a coloring book with his little daughter but he looked up when he saw Diosa. He followed her. Their eyes met.

"What's with that?" I said.

"Fleeting," she said.

"Like a boat fleet?"

"On TV he's got writers."

"Is he a poet now?"

"Better than most. He takes private workshops with David St. John," Diosa said.

"Maybe his writers should take workshops with David St. John."

"They have Stanford MFA's. Who do you think writes teleplays?" she said.

Frankly, I never think about who writes teleplays. But we were speaking pretty quietly because people sit around in these cafes with their laptops open and if you say anything witty it ends up on a TV show in a couple weeks. I've practically spoken whole episodes of *House* or *Boston Legal* or *SNL*.

We ordered lunch, which Diosa didn't eat. I ate all of mine. She grew pale, her breathing labored. Then she gasped, "I have to go back now."

Out we went, rounding the corner to the drug store where the clerk said, "No, they haven't called it in."

Diosa collapsed. I got her to a chair.

"She can't breathe for Christ's sake," I said.

"I'll call again," the clerk said. "Their line's still busy," she said.

"I'm going over there," I said.

"Give them five minutes more," Diosa gasped. She smiled calmly and inauthentically. Diosa was dangerous when this sweet in a crisis. Somebody would pay. Heads would roll and it could be anybody's.

"Nurse Alvara is a controlling bitch," I said.

The clerk called again.

"I'm going," I said. Now I had to pee. At the moment when my swift action was most needed, I had to pee. I held it. Walked across the parking lot, across the street, into the plaza and up the stairs to the doctor's office. When the nurses at the desk saw me, sensing true desperation, they got up and ran away. I peered around the waiting room where one old woman sat, blonde hair a straggle, lipstick all over her face. I bent over the reception counter. Looked down the hall.

"My wife can't breathe!" I yelled. "My wife can't breathe!" I waited. "My wife can't breathe! My wife can't breathe! My wife can't breathe! I'm coming in!"

Nurse Alvara, the biggest one, came out.

"My wife, your patient, Diosa, is sitting in the pharmacy gasping for breath, waiting for someone to call in a prescription," I said.

"Let me talk to the doctor," Nurse Alvara said.

"What have you been doing for the last three hours?" I said. "Call in the prescription."

Nurse Alvara got up and left.

"Call in the prescription! Call in the prescription! Call in the prescription!" I yelled over and over and over and over until Nurse Alvara came back out.

"I'm calling in the prescription now," Nurse Alvara said.

Nurse Alvara looked at me and I looked at Nurse Alvara.

"I'm calling it in now," she said.

"I'm waiting," I said.

She picked up the phone. Held it to her ear. She looked at me. Finally, she lifted her right index finger and tapped a button. I heard the clerk on the other end of the line.

Back in the drug store Diosa was sitting in Gary Busey's lap sucking on a Ventolin.

"I love this woman," said Gary Busey.

"I was too weak to fight him off," said Diosa. "And he lent me his Ventolin."

"I'm in love," said Busey. "This is my favorite woman."

"You'll need a poetry workshop," I told him.

I wrestled Diosa from his arms, got Diosa in my truck and headed back down the coast.

Diosa took two hard hits on her new cartridge of Ventolin. She took several deep breaths. Rolled down her window and took in the moist, ocean air. "It's really frightening when you can't breathe," she said. She reached into her purse and pulled out her pack of Parliament 100's and lit up.

So now Diosa was sick and I had to sub for her in her poetry workshop at La-La Holy.

Me and You
By Patricia

A million girls were kissed tonight
But only one was kissed by you
A hundred thousand bodies touched just right
But only we were just two
Ten thousand arms grabbed each other tight
But our love was overdue
A thousand boys said "I love you" this night
But I heard mine from you
A hundred couples shared our plight
But they weren't like me and you
Ten more had a horrible fight
But you and I stayed true
And then there was just two
Me and you.
A million
A hundred thousand
Ten thousand
A thousand
A hundred
Ten
And two.
Me and you.

"It's shaped like an H-Bomb," I said.

"A top," said somebody.

"No, a balloon."

"A tree."

"Wait!" I said. Clearly I'd taken the discussion in the wrong direction. "Has Diosa ever said anything to you about not rhyming?"

Everyone in the class looked down and away like my dog, HD, after she broke into the trash.

I sat in front of fifteen young dog poets.

"Were you young poets in the trash?" I said. "Were you young poets finding poems in the trash? Bad poets! Bad poets!" I said.

"Are you saying something is wrong?" Patrica said.

"Meter?" I said. "Foot? Poetic forms? Blank verse? Free? Have you naughty poets ever heard of these things?"

The young poets looked behind them as if something were sneaking up on them.

"Look at me, you naughty poets," I said. "Stay out of the trash!"

"Are we having a culture bias thing here," said Patricia, "because this is how my people write poetry."

"What people are those?" I said.

"My people," said Patricia.

"People who don't know anything?"

"Black people."

"You're not black," I said. "You're Irish."

"Careful, Professor Shark," someone said. "You're violating her comfort zone."

"I want to be black. I can be whatever I want," Patricia said.

"Okay, what if I give you that. So writers like Quincy Troupe, Jay Wright, Rita Dove kind of people?"

"Who are they?" said Patricia.

"Poets?" I suggested.

"Maya Angelou," Patricia said.

"She has a greeting card line," someone said.

"She has a greeting card line?"

"I think she does," someone else said.

"She doesn't write them, she's quoted on them," said another young poet.

"Good fences make good neighbors," I said.

"Like that."

"The road less traveled," I said.

"Yeah," said somebody. "Like that."

"And that," I said, holding my head, "makes all the difference."

Later I rewarded myself by dropping by Gabriela and Mingo's on my way home. They lived so close to LAX you could wave to the passengers as the planes landed.

"I cannot believe she did not tell you," Gabriela said. She put cheese on the table in front of me. Hot bread.

Mingo brought out bourbon. "You look like you need to get right to the liquor," he said.

"She made for you one of those, how do you say, traps for boobies," said Gabriela.

"Booby trap," I said.

"A WMD" said Mingo.

"Where are the WMDs?" I said.

"In your classroom," said Gabriela.

"I think they have microphones in the crucifixes," I said.

"Drink some bourbon," said Mingo.

"I'm going to write a poem," I said.

"Don't do it," said Mingo. "You'll regret it the rest of your life."

"So the goddess is feeling pretty sick," said Gabriela.

"She called," said Mingo.

"While you were trapping boobies in her class," Gabriela said.

"She shouldn't smoke cigarettes with a chest infection and asthma," I said.

"They aren't related," said Mingo.

"They're just together," I said. I drank my bourbon. "In her chest."

Mingo poured me some more. We ate the bread and cheese. "What are you going to do?" Mingo said, "Say something?"

THE LIFE OF JESUS IN
LOS ANGELES: THE EARLY YEARS

IT WAS DRESS AS YOUR Favorite Person Day at Palisades High School. Everybody who dressed as their favorite person went up on stage and talked about their favorite person and how they were dressed just like their favorite person. (You could probably write this yourself, but let me write it for you). Jesus wore a black, multi-layered, multi-length gauze skirt, a short, tight pink David Bowie t-shirt that showed her belly button, a little black sweater with a huge, black, fake-fur collar, five inch platform heels. Her hair was shoulder length, purple, black, red, pink, and yellow. She wore a button that said, "Fuck art, let's dance."

"Who are you?" someone yelled.

"I'm Jesus," she said.

There was some cheering among the hippie-types, her disciples, but a lot more booing.

"Blessed are the cheese-makers," Jesus said.

When the populace began to throw things, the Assistant Principle, Mrs. Davenport, escorted Jesus off the stage.

"This was a mistake," said Mrs. Davenport.

"They make the same mistake every time," Jesus said.

(JESUS CONFOUNDS THE WISE PEOPLE)

That afternoon I picked up Jesus at the bus stop.

"Mrs. Davenport called today," I said.

Jesus moved over closer to the passenger door.

"You were nominated for Academic All-America," I said to her.

"They just want you to buy the book," said Jesus. "If you buy the book, you get in. If you don't buy the book, you don't."

"You don't buy the book," I said.

"Can I spend the money on shoes?"

"You turned down membership to the Math Club."

"I'm Vice President of the India Club," said Jesus. "Ashley said she'd teach me to belly dance."

"Your biology, history, and English teachers say they want you for Academic Decathlon," I said.

"Really, Father, competition? I'm thinking about a nose piercing and a sitar," said Jesus.

"You don't think it's kind of an honor?" I said.

"To compete against a bunch of people who think they know something?" Jesus said.

(THE LOAVES AND FISHES)

Next morning, when I drove Jesus to school, there was a peace rally against the American invasions of everywhere. There were a few teachers and a bunch of students on the corner with signs that said things like WAR IS NOT THE ANSWER.

"Look," said Jesus to me. "A peace rally. Right up my alley."

"Or down your alley."

I pulled to the curb and all of the students at the peace rally ran toward her yelling, "Jesus! Jesus!"

"I thought everybody was upset that you called yourself Jesus," I said.

Jesus turned to me. "They've recently had a change of heart," she said.

"Do you have any idea why?"

"I'll die for their sins?" Jesus said.

Jesus jumped out of the car and turned to the crowd and raised her hands above her head. "Bless you all!" Jesus said.

"Tell us a story, Jesus," someone yelled, and then everyone began yelling, "Tell us a story! Tell us a story!"

"Don't make them late for class, Jesus," said an older man.

"This is the story of Hansel and Gretel," Jesus said to the crowd.

"You! You!" screamed the crowd.

"No, Hansel and Gretel," said Jesus

Those on the edges grabbed passers-by and said, "Jesus is telling a story! Jesus is telling a story!"

Jesus spoke and the crowd grew.

"Once upon a time," Jesus said, "in Germany in the 1940's there were two little German children named Hansel and Gretel."

Okay, you know that story. The only real difference here is that there are two evil witches and their names are Hitler and Mussolini and after Hansel and Gretel escape they travel to America where they live out their days writing many poems and novels which never get published.

"You can't end there, Jesus!" someone yelled.

"Nothing ever ends," said Jesus.

"Huzzah!" said the crowd. "You! You! You!" shouted the crowd. "Huzzah for Jesus, Daughter of God!" They put Jesus on their shoulders and carried her into the school.

That afternoon a call came in over my phone.

"Hello, this is Mrs. Davenport, Assistant Principal at Palisades High School," the voice on the machine said, "and I'd like to speak to you about your daughter, Jesus."

I picked up.

"Is this Jesus' father?" said Mrs. Davenport.

"That's a hard one to answer," I said. "Okay, let's start with yes."

"Did you order lox, cream cheese, and two thousand bagels and have them delivered here at lunch time today?"

"I probably didn't," I said.

"Jerry's Deli?" said Mrs. Davenport.

"I've been there," I said. "But a lot of people have."

"The power went out this morning. The cafeteria closed," said Mrs. Davenport. "There was no food. Then the lox and bagels showed up."

"And you think Jesus was involved?" I said.

"Her name was on the receipt," said Mrs. Davenport. "I asked her who paid and she said her father."

"Did she mention God?" I said.

"God?"

"God the Father," I said.

"Her Heavenly father," Mrs. Davenport said. "It was a very nice thing to say about you. And as long as you're aware, we're appreciative, but there are procedures for these kinds of things."

"Undoubtedly," I said.

(SHE WALKS WITH ME AND SHE TALKS WITH ME)

I picked up Jesus at the Elementary School where the bus left off the Topanga high school kids who went to Pali High. I could spot her through the bus window because she was the only one with black, red, blonde, chartreuse hair. She wore tight jeans and black platform boots that made her six feet tall, a tight tiny-checked tweed jacket, a round, black felt fedora with a single peacock feather in the front sticking straight up.

She crossed the parking lot and got onto the back of my motorcycle. "Hello Father," she said.

"Hello daughter," I said. "Permission to speak freely?"

"Certainly Father," Jesus said.

"Did you perform a miracle today?"

"A miracle?"

"At school," I said. I clutched and headed down School Road toward the traffic light.

"I simply got everyone to share," Jesus said.

"Two thousand bagels," I said.

"Was it that many?" said Jesus.

"Who paid?" I said.

"Paid?" Jesus said.

"There was a receipt with your name on it," I said. I pulled onto the Canyon Boulevard and into downtown, past the crystal shop with peace flags, the flower shop, the Inn of the Seventh Ray, past several crosses bedecked with flowers where the most recent road victims had departed for eternally safer roads.

"That bill goes to me," I said to Jesus.

"Oh Father," said Jesus, "it's probably tax deductible."

"Why not send the bill to Serum?" I said. "He's rich."

"Where's the miracle there?" said Jesus.

I pulled into my drive and parked beneath the lowest retaining wall.

"I'm in a new band," Jesus said to me. She'd been in a rock band with five other girls. The band's name was Jesus, Shakespeare and Hitler. Every kid in Los Angeles is in a rock band. Then they get older and become poets, though some become actors and then become poets.

"*Les Gods*," Jesus said.

"Don't tell me," I said.

"Aphrodite. Buddha."

"Buddha wasn't a god," I said.

"Elvis. That blue dude."

"Krishna?"

"Yeah, that's him," Jesus said. "Hari-hari."

"Could we cool the miracles?" I said. "Just do free miracles."

"People love me," Jesus said.

"You feed them, they love you," I said.

"It's amazing how people love me," said Jesus.

(JESUS HEALS THE ROCK STAR)

David Bowie didn't know if he could face the audience that night at the Wiltern. Something had taken hold of his veins and his bones. His face was hot. His arm pits swelled. But if his voice held. If his voice held.

"You don't look so good, David," said his guitarist, Mazeen.

"Well, it's not always all about looks you know," said Bowie. "What do you say we give it a go?"

You can do it a million times and it's always frightening and exhilarating and boring, too. That's why you need cocaine. The stage is bathed in light, the auditorium a noisy, black sea. Bowie looked out, his stomach turning. He felt fluid in his throat. His bones felt brittle and black. His head ached. His knees shook. But looking down, there in front him, at the foot of the stage, stood a girl. She wore tight pants and platform shoes that made her look six feet tall, a short, plaid jacket; her hair, red and yellow and black and deep blue and blonde, poured out from under a felt derby from which, like the eye of God, protruded a peacock feather, straight and tall. He stared at the feather. He stared at the feather. He put out his hand and she reached up and touched it. Then he felt like a rocket had hit him in the chest. And then he felt fine. In fact, he felt as good as he'd ever felt in his life.

The next day the LA Times, after a rave review, quoted Bowie relating the incident. "It was quite amazing really," he said.

"Did you find out who she was?"

"You wouldn't really want to find out who she was now, would you?" Bowie said. "I mean, even if you could?"

Diosa handed the Calendar Section to me at breakfast. Jesus came out of her room, dressed for school, with fifteen minutes allotted to put on her make-up.

"I guess you touched David Bowie last night," I said to Jesus.

"Yes," Jesus said. "It was wonderful."

TWO LITTLE TERRORISTS
FROM LA BOCA

(SUNG TO "DIAMONDS ARE A GIRL'S BEST FRIEND"
OR "THE LITTLE OLD LADY FROM PASADENA")

"I WANT BIG TITS," said Gabriela. "You promised me big tits."

"I don't remember promising you big tits," I said.

"You promised Mingo a sail boat and you promised me big tits. You gave him his sail boat in your last book."

"He made me gay," said Mingo.

"Big tits?" I said.

"You promised them," Gabriela said. "I want them."

Diosa yawned. "I don't even like tits. Tits are a pain."

"Like the rich saying money is meaningless," Gabriela said.

I took the water pipe from Mingo. "You high yet?" I said.

"I don't know," said Mingo. "Maybe I'm too drunk. I cannot feel it."

I took a long hit and held it for a while. Released. "You smoked seventy bucks worth of pot, you should feel it or stop," I said to Mingo. I looked at Gabriela's breasts. "You've got fine tits," I said.

"These are nothing," she said, holding them from underneath. "I have nothing."

Mingo reached for the Blantons bourbon, removed the horse statue cork, poured himself a double. He raised an eye at me and I pushed my glass forward. Mingo filled it. "I would have thought," he said, "with the children, well, you know."

"Not another word from you," Gabriela said.

Mingo shrugged deeply, his eyes drooping salaciously toward Diosa.

"You couldn't even get it up," Diosa said to him.

"I could try."

"He ees old, but he ees weeling," I said.

"Soon I will be dead," Mingo said.

"Don't you dare talk of death after all you've been through," said Gabriela. "Anyway, we are talking tits here."

Anyway, it was late, after three a.m. on Thanksgiving Day night. The four of us sat on bar chairs around a high, round, iron table that Diosa made during her welding phase. Across the way, friends slept in the Tiki-Tiki room on a futon, upstairs more sleepers, Mingo and Gabriela's kids, Eva and Anahi, a young, Armenian writer named Kardashian, Jesus and some boyfriend. I didn't know his name but I called him James the Lesser.

The corner where we sat had two yellow walls, a window in one of them looking out to a portico where a small, round, tiled Moroccan table and two similar chairs sat on red brick under a fruit bearing avocado tree; under the tree a statue of the sitting Buddha surrounded by sea shells, an Australian fern, and hanging on the barn-wood wall behind, a metal candelabra, a cow skull from Rosarito, a ceramic Mexican sun, a metal painted fish, a white crescent moon from The Strip in Pittsburgh, and in a flat, gray frieze, the head of the Virgin tilted right, eyes downcast.

Inside, on one side of the square window, a painting of a couple, smoking, poised in tango *tete-et-tete* that Diosa bought in La Boca when she and Gabriela and me gave readings in Buenos Aires. On the other side of the window, a print of a horse head, a mare, entitled *Etena*, numbered 8/35 and signed by the artist Solozar Ama, a gift Diosa bought for me in Oaxaca. On the other yellow wall hung a red poncho with a black collar and two thick, black, vertical stripes, black fringe along its edges; the uniform of the Argentinean Montoneros, Gabriela and Mingo's revolutionary army.

After reading at the Centro de Cultural in San Telmo, a borough of Buenos Aires, Gabriela took Diosa and me to dinner at Parrilla Al Carbon with a half dozen *desaparecidos*, survivors, like Gabriela, of Argentina's war against its own. The restaurant opened at eleven at night, though the place didn't begin to fill up till one a.m. We sat around a long table, two huge trays of grilled beef and bottles of red wine. A young illustrator, Carlitos, who spent a year and a half in jail because of his association with Mingo, gave me the poncho, and a bayonet used during the Argentinean invasion of the Islas de Malvinas, the British Falklands. The bayonet had four red stripes on its handle.

"British soldiers?" I said.

"*Ovejas*," said Gabriela. "Sheep. It is against Argentinean military policy to kill other armed men."

Carlitos gave me that bayonet, and the poncho of the Montoneros, because I was Mingo's friend. Carlitos called Mingo, Comandante. Mingo spent four years on death row, survived a year of torture without giving up a single name. Now, anywhere I went in the world, if a survivor found out I was a friend of Mingo's, I received gifts.

Above the collar of the poncho, Diosa hung the medallion of the Mothers of the disappeared. She'd welded the slogan of the disappeared on a plate of iron and given it to Gabriela not long after we all first met: *Ni olvida. Ni perdon.* Never forgive. Never forget.

"We never kidnapped or killed anyone in front of their family," Mingo said.

"It was a war," said Gabriela.

"That we lost," Mingo said.

"They had tanks and automatic weapons," said Gabriea. "I didn't even know how to use my gun." She pushed her glass forward for more bourbon. "Do I get my tits now?"

"You got'em," I said.

AT THE UNIVERSITY OF LA-LA HOLY: THE TRAFFIC OF UNICORNS

(It Might Be An Arcane Allusion But Is Most Likely Just Something I Made Up That Rhymed With The Tropic of Capricorn, Because Originally I Had Written Down The Tropic Of Cancer, Because That Was What I Wanted To Write About, Although, Now That I've Written It Down, You Could Look At It Like the List of Ships In The Iliad And Watch Them Parading By In A Line and Think, Hmm, Like So Many Unicorns Parading By, One Unicorn After Another Just Walking On By; It Just Might Get You Thinking About Titles And Authors As If They Were So Many Unicorns (You See, I Don't Believe In Authors, Barely Believe In Titles, Almost Believe In Unicorns); Yet, By Now, I See The End Of This Section Dovetailing Under Its Title Like A Tailing Dove; When Accident Feels Like Prescience, Maybe It Is Prescience)

MILLER HENRY WEI WAS tall, about six-three, wore horned-rim glasses and a black flat-top haircut. He looked like a scientist, but instead he was an English major at the U of La-La Holy. He had a lot of geek in him, in fact, he'd once been a scientist, but he was smart enough that when he took Intro to Poetry from Diosa he got bedazzled. Of course, he fell in love with her and lucky for him he was just a big geeky nuisance and not a handsome, poetic Shelley Keats type or I'd have killed him. Like a lot of kids at the U of La-La Holy, Miller was really majoring in me and Diosa; he'd become passionate about writing and literature, read like crazy, took things too literally and understood little of what he read; he was prime to really learn something but now had to take a lot of required classes filled with indolent and ignorant dummies, nice kids who for the most part didn't give a shit. Miller was like one of those fourth graders who read all the time but didn't know how to read anything. "Hey Professor Shark," said Miller Henry Wei when I walked into class that day.

"Hey Shark, he called you Professor Shark!" yelled Tanya Tyzinski.

"Just don't call me late for lunch," I said,

"Why not?" said Miller Henry Wei.

"Because it's an ancient Eisenhower joke," said I.

"I don't get it."

"Eisenhower late for lunch," I said.

"Who's Eisenhower? said Tanya Tyzinski.

"You're conflating two different jokes," said Wil Deeth, a lawyer who was older than me but who had returned to La-La Holy to rectify his having flunked out thirty-five years ago. ("What do you think of that?" he'd asked me. "You're nuts," I said. "My advisor told me not to take you," said Wil Deeth, "that no one can understand what you're saying." "Do you understand me?" I said. "I think I do," said Wil. "Well?" I said. "Am I nuts?" said Wil). Wil was a little nuts. He wore big glasses and had a full head of hair. He was Catholic and still married to his first wife. He wore a coat and tie to class because he came straight from the office and he always apologized for it. His casual clothes were even worse. "I like the coat and tie," I told him. "Really?" said Wil. "Never ask me 'really?'" I said.

"One's a knock-knock joke where 'Eisenhower late for lunch' is the answer to 'Eisenhower who?' And the other ends, 'You can call me anything, just don't call me late for lunch,'" Wil said.

"Whew," said Tanya Tyzinski. "Can we go home now?"

"Did I tell you guys about the Korean kid who threatened to kill me in class?" I said.

"Yes," moaned the class.

"Taking acid and driving my motorcycle?"

"Yeeesss Doctor Shark," the class droned.

"You guys really know me," I said.

"They're lying about all of that," said Miller Henry Wei.

"Who's Eisenhower?" said Tanya Tyzinski.

"You should take advantage of this, Professor Shark," said Miller Henry Wei. "Tanya wants to know something."

"Do you know the whole 'late for lunch' joke?" I asked Wil.

"I'll have to look it up," said Wil.

"This is the funnest class," said Jimbo Giles.

"Professor Shark, I heard you're writing *The Last Book of Everything*," said Miller Henry Wei. "But I think Henry Miller already wrote *The Last Book of Everything*."

"He stole it from me," I said.

"How is that possible?" said Wil.

"He was a plagiarist," I said.

"I thought you didn't believe in time travel," said Miller Henry Wei.

"I don't," I said, "but I believe in plagiarism."

"Can we plagiarize?" asked Tanya Tyzinski.

"Can you?" I said.

"Can we plagiarize in here?"

"Can you plagiarize out of here?"

"This is the funnest class," said Jimbo Giles. The other twenty kids were doing homework, talking on cell phones, Facebooking on their laptops or i-phones.

"Besides, I'm not writing *The Last Book of Everything*. I'm in *The Last Book of Everything*."

"What's it about?" said Wil.

"Everything," I said.

"Am I in it?" said Tanya.

"You bet," I said.

"Hurray, I'm in a book!" said Jimbo Giles. "Wait till I tell my mother."

"Don't tell your mother," I said to him.

You can see why I was such a popular teacher. My philosophy of education had really changed over the years. I never lectured and I never asked a question I already knew the answer to. Students lined up for blocks to register for my courses. If they didn't get in, then they sat in. They brought their friends. Kids came from other schools, other cities, other states. Other professors listened outside my door. They hated me. I was never nominated for teaching awards, but I was the fourth leading Los Angeles area tourist attraction after Disneyland, Universal City, and Venice Beach, just ahead of Melrose Avenue, Hollywood, the Santa Monica Promenade, the Pier, Abbot Kinney Blvd. and well ahead of Lego Land and Disney's California Adventure.

Anyway, I'm not writing *The Last Book of Everything* I'm only pretending to write it to create a myth about myself that would entice movie interest.

And it did. Now there's a documentary about me called *The Last Book of Everything* when it's not called *The Death of Writing in America* whichever comes first.

"So," I said, "what class is this?"

"It's The Language of Fiction," said Jimbo Giles, "and this is Tuesday."

"That's great, Jimbo. Did anybody read 'A Good Man Is Hard to Find,'" I asked.

Henry Miller Wei raised his hand and so did Wil. That was it.

"How about that grandmother!" I said.

"Professor Shark, you better check out Henry Miller," said Miller Henry Wei.

It was this morning, on our way to the Post Office, that we gave the book its final imprimatur. We have evolved a new cosmogony of literature, Boris and I. It is to be a new Bible—*The Last Book*. All who have anything to say will say it here—*anonymously*. We will exhaust the age. After us not another book—not for a generation, at least. Heretofore we had been digging in the dark, with nothing but instinct to guide us. Now we shall have a vessel in which to pour the vital fluid, a bomb which, when we throw it, will set off the world. We shall put into it enough to give the writers of tomorrow their plots, their dramas, their poems, their myths, their sciences. The world will be able to feed on it for a thousand years to come. It is colossal in its pretentiousness. The thought of it almost shatters us. For a hundred years or more the world, *our* world, has been dying. And not one man, in these last hundred years or so, has been crazy enough to put a bomb up the asshole of creation and set it off. The world is rotting away, dying piecemeal. But it needs the *coup de grace*, it needs to be blown to smithereens. Not one of us is intact, and yet we have in us all the continents and the seas between the continents and the birds of the air. We are going to put it down—the evolution of this world which has died but which has not been buried. We are swimming on the face of time and all else has drowned, is drowning, or will drown. It will be enormous, the Book. There will be oceans of space in which to move

117

about, to perambulate, to sing, to dance, to climb, to bathe, to leap somersaults, to whine, to rape, to murder. A cathedral, a veritable cathedral, in the building of which everybody will assist who had lost his identity. There will be masses for the dead, prayers, confessions, hymns, a moaning and chattering, a sort of murderous insouciance; there will be rose windows and gargoyles and acolytes and pallbearers. You can bring your horses in and gallop through the aisles. You can butt your head against the walls – they won't give. You can pray in any language you choose, or you can curl up outside and go to sleep. It will last a thousand years, at least, this cathedral, and there will be no replica, for the builders will be dead and the formula, too. We will have postcards made and organize tours. We will build a town around it and set up a free commune. We have no need for genius—genius is dead. We have need for strong hands, for spirits who are willing to give up the ghost and put on flesh . . .

—*Tropic of Cancer*, Henry Miller

Unfortunately, he wasn't kidding. I wonder if that's where Ray Carver got his idea for *Cathedral*. And LA's own Charles Bukowski. "Genius?" said Bukowski. "Tolstoy, Chekhov? I don't see it. Give me a good beer shit."

HOSTAGE:
A HOLLYWOOD PARABLE

HOSTAGE
HOSTAGE, LLC
5300 MELROSE AVE.
WEST BLDG. 2ND FLOOR
HOLLYWOOD, CA. 90038Z
(312)960-4570 / (323)960-4571 FAX

JAN. 14, 2010

Dear Neighbors,

We will be filming scenes for the feature film "Hostage" at Country Foods Market 415 S. Topanga Cyn. Blvd. on Jan. 22nd & 23rd. "Hostage" is a police drama and this scene involves a robbery at the market and the subsequent police investigation of the robbery. There will be some single shot gunfire but no explosions or late night filming.

We have applied for all the necessary film permits and will follow all specific guidelines for the area. We are requesting limited traffic control while we are filming to help ensure that residence (sic) and business patrons can smoothly get to where they need to go. We will make every effort not to disturb you. We appreciate your hospitality and cooperation while we are filming in your neighborhood.

If you have any questions or concerns regarding our filming activities, feel free to call us or drop by and see us during the filming. Thank you for supporting the film industry and keeping our jobs, and economic contribution to the community here in Southern California.

Sincerely,

Scott Poole
(310) 901-5114 cellSteve Nelson
(818) 999-7510 voicemail/pager
(310) 350-2289 cell

The Hostage Location Department

I found that in my gate at four o'clock, along with a **COUNTY & CITY OF LOS ANGELES FILMING SURVEY**, a form which pretty much reiterated the letter, except I was supposed to sign it having filled out one of these three boxes:

__ **I HAVE NO CONCERNS regarding the proposed activities.**
__ **MY CONCERNS with the proposed filming activities are:**

_____
__ **I HAVE NO CONCERNS but prefer not to sign my name.**

At six o'clock someone rang the bell outside my fence. The dogs ignited, charged down the stairs through the kitchen and pounded out the door. When I peered over my balcony railing, HD stood about three feet from the gate saying "Groof! Groof!" while Piccolo threw himself at the gate, wham, wham, wham, arf, arf arf. It could scare the shit out of you if you weren't familiar with it. It was winter, already dark, so I turned on the floodlight and peered over my balcony.

"Who is it?"

"Hostage?" came a small voice.

"You better go down there, Shark," said Diosa.

"Yeah, Shark, you better go down there," said Jesus.

So I went down there. I held Piccolo by the collar, opened the gate, threw Piccolo back inside, slammed the gate. A little guy with a balding crew cut, wire-rimmed glasses, stood there with a clip board. He wore khakis and an argyle, sleeveless sweater-vest over a button down. He looked in his mid-twenties. A Production Assistant, right?

"Did you sign your form?" said the little guy.

"I just got it," I said.

"Garroof!" said HD.

Piccolo slammed against the gate.

"I'm glad I didn't go in there," said the little guy.

"We're all glad," I said.

"I need the form tonight," said the little guy. "We start shooting tonight."

"I just got it," I said.

"So you have no concerns and prefer not to sign."

"No," I said. "I have concerns and prefer not to sign."

"There's no box for that," the little guy said.

"Exactly."

"What are your concerns?"

"My concerns are that something is going to happen that I'm not concerned about yet," I said, "but then I'll have already signed off."

"There's really no place for that," said the little guy.

"Don't I know it," I said.

Just then Piccolo hit the gate and popped it open. In a bound his nose was in the guy's eyes. The little Hollywood guy jumped back and down a step. I caught Piccolo in the air by the collar. He dangled there for a moment, then I threw him back inside and slammed the gate. Undeterred, Piccolo the idiot began slamming against the gate again.

"I'm concerned one of my dogs will get out and bite somebody," I said. "And not this one, but the other dangerous one."

"Heh-heh," said the little guy.

"I'm concerned somebody will try to steal one of my cats."

"Oh no," said Hollywood.

"They do it every time." I said. "I have to go on set and get my cat back. And there's sewer construction a hundred yards north of here shutting the road down to one lane, now you'll be clogging things up a hundred yards south."

"I don't think there's enough space for all these concerns," said the little man.

"You guys will park in front of my driveway and I won't be able to get in or out. And this place will be swarming with fat, worthless cops."

The little guy began to walk sideways down the steps.

"I'm concerned that something bad I haven't even thought of will happen!" I yelled over the barking.

The little man left. I went inside. "I didn't fill in any boxes," I said to Diosa.

"They usually have a box for that," she said.

"I hate Hollywood."

"You hate everything."

"I like my kitties," I said.

"You like your kitties," said Diosa.

"I like you," I said.

"But we're ambivalent about you," said Jesus.

"You love everybody," I said to Jesus.

"But not you, Father," said Jesus. "You don't make enough money."

"Why don't you get a part-time job?" said Diosa.

"Life is my part-time job," I said.

"It would get you out of the house," Diosa said.

"You know," said Jesus, "I'm trying to watch TV and I can barely hear my own complaining."

"I get out of the house," I said.

"Not enough," said Diosa. "You're a huge presence, even when you're not here."

"So I should not be here less?" I said.

"Father," said Jesus, "you seldom make any sense!"

"He's slightly autistic, dear," Diosa said to Jesus.

Just then my favorite cat, Mucha Plata, bounced into the living room.

"Shit," said Diosa, "she's got a live rat."

Mucha Plata looked at Diosa. She looked at me. She dropped the rat and it ran under the TV cabinet. "Urple," said Mucha Plata.

Three other cats appeared out of nowhere and folded up around the cabinet.

"This is the problem," I said to Mucha Plata. "You're supposed to keep the rats out."

"Breep?" said Mucha Plata.

Every once in a while one of the other cats, Yoko Dodo, Meesh, or

Cheese, got up, walked around the cabinet, then reached under. There'd be some screeching and rustling, then the cat backed away and lay down again. They took turns. The cats watched the rat. The two dogs watched the cats.

"Looks like we're in for the long haul," I said.

"There's too many fucking animals in here," Diosa said. "What are they shooting up the street?"

"A hold up," I said. "The movie's called Hostage."

"Car chases?"

"Just guns."

"You must do something, Father," Jesus said. "I can't sleep with a rat in here."

I got up and moved the TV off the cabinet. I moved the VCR, DVD, and satellite box. I opened the porch door so the rat could run out. Then I lifted the cabinet. The rat jumped straight up, as if trying to climb the wall. When he came back down the cats were still there. The rat stood up on his hind legs. The cats didn't budge. I could see that the rodent was already pretty tired. He had saliva all over him. Mucha Plata had already run him around pretty good before she brought him in. A present for me. It made it easier for an idiot like me to catch him.

"Poor thing," said Diosa. "Save him."

"For what?" I said.

"She brought him for you," said Diosa.

So I put on my thick wood-stove gloves. I grabbed the rat, took it outside, and let it go over the fence into the vacant lot. Our calico, Music Batty, dropped off the porch roof and pounced on the rat.

I came back in. The other four cats hadn't moved. I put everything back together.

"Music Batty got him," I said.

"Did you shut the door?" said Jesus.

"Music never comes in," I said.

"Just rats," said Jesus.

"Topanga gig. The fat cops will be eating croissants instead of donuts," Diosa said.

And lo, came Hollywood. They parked in front of my driveway, their trucks rumbling in the pre-dawn. Their guns went bang and bang, the dogs threw themselves against the fence and there was the weeping and gnashing of traffic, especially at rush hour whence the commuters who had come unto the wilderness for a short cut honked and raged against their helplessness. They were going to be late for the jobs they hated!

Down the road, someone trying to pass the line of waiting cars crossed the double yellow line into the opposing traffic and smacked head on into another car.

Soon our fire truck wailed onto the Boulevard. The paramedics followed. The actors cheered them and waved. A helicopter broke over the distant hills. The innocent driver was crushed under her steering wheel and died. The other driver, a guy, was already drunk, or still drunk. Another cross on the road. For a while, flowers. Four CHP patrol cars and three motor cycles were parked in the Topanga Antique Store parking lot next to my house. Eleven state troopers alternately strolled to the Mimosa Café and, as Diosa predicted, ate croissants. They were not traffic police. They were movie escorts, here to create traffic, not ease it. And indeed, our cat, the Cheese, went missing. And I couldn't leave my house without walking down to the Country Foods Market, finding the production manager, and begging him to move his trucks out of my carport.

"Why?" he said. "You got somewhere to go?"

At least it wasn't like in Venice Beach where the police escorted the actors off the set to buy crack, but that's another parable.

AT THE UNIVERSITY OF LA-LA HOLY: THE PERFECT STAIN

EVERY WEEK OR SO I threw out my mail, erased my email, and skipped quickly through my phone messages at the U of La-La Holy. Usually, it was too late to do anything about any of it. But that morning Blind Ray Hynde, the Department Chair, left a message for me to come see him. Blind Ray couldn't see or teach, so they made him Chair. I published ten books and had a thousand students following me around, so they wanted me outta there.

I called. "Can't we just talk on the phone?" I said.

"No," said Ray.

I didn't know why I had to have a face-to-face talk with Blind Ray because Blind Ray couldn't see me anyways, but I walked the ten feet down to Blind Ray's office.

"Come in and shut the door," said Blind Ray Hynde.

I thought maybe if I just shut the door but then didn't go in, Blind Ray wouldn't notice and would just talk to the air for a while, because Blind Ray really liked to talk, then if it was really important Blind Ray would bring it up again later.

"Sit down," said Blind Ray.

I sat down.

"You've got some trouble," Ray said.

"Trouble," I said.

"A student is complaining."

"One student?"

"I'm afraid so. You didn't happen to use the N-Word in class the other day."

"An n-word," I said.

"*The* N-Word," said Blind Ray Hynde.

"Nice?" I said.

"No," said Blind Ray.

"Gnosis?" I said. "Sometimes people think that's an n-word."

"No," said Blind Ray.

"Narcissism?"

"No."

"Necrophilia?"

"No," Blind Ray said.

"Nous?"

"No."

"Nigel?"

"No."

"Napa?"

"No," said Blind Ray.

"Necessary," I said. "Sometimes they don't like being told they have to do stuff."

"No."

"Knowledge? That's a tricky one sometimes," I said.

"No," said Blind Ray. "It was racial."

"Nigeria? Nippon? Nappy? "

"No," Ray said.

"What?" I said. .

"*The* N-Word," said Blind Ray Hynde.

"What n-word?" I said.

"The N-Word!" said Blind Ray Hynde.

"But I have to guess?" I said.

"It was Patricia D'Aneesha," said Blind Ray.

"Patricia," I said. "O'Doul. I don't know have a D'Aneesha."

"She's black."

"Not Irish?"

"She's black now. And in your class."

"She's not in my class. She's in Diosa's class."

"You said it in a class."

"I thought there was something fishy at Thanksgiving when she showed up with that cheap rum drink."

"She was at your house for Thanksgiving?"

"Her whole family," I said. "Daughter, sister, that Islamist guy she's hanging with now. He was black."

"She married him," said Blind Ray Hynde.

"Sweet," I said.

"Shark," said Blind Ray Hynde. "Patricia has gone to the Grievance Committee, the Chair of African-American Studies, the Head of Cultural Affairs, and to the Dean. She wants you fired for saying the N-Word in class."

"Holy smokes," I said.

"She cried right here in front of me."

"You could hear her crying," I said.

"She's been crying everywhere."

"I guess she's doing a lot of crying," I said.

"Would you talk to her?" asked Blind Ray.

"Of course I'll talk to her," I said.

"Well, she doesn't want to talk to you," said Ray.

"That will make it harder to talk to her," I said.

"The Dean is afraid she's going to go public and sue the school," said Blind Ray Hynde.

"Are you afraid, Ray?" I said.

"Everyone is afraid," Blind Ray Hynde said.

"Everyone," I said.

"Even your former friends and colleagues," said Blind Ray blindly.

"What former friends and colleagues?" I said. "Over some n-word?"

"*The* N-word," said Blind Ray.

"They should be afraid of Patricia," I said.

"They're afraid of you."

"You wouldn't want to tell me what it is, would you?"

"It's too heinous," Ray said.

"Nebuchadrezzar," I said. "Ninny. Nincompoop. Nazi. Nietzsche. Nasty. Knack. No, not knack. Did I say narcoleptic yet?"

"I think you better make an appointment with the Dean," said Blind Ray Hynde.

"Is there an n-word for abortion?" I said. "I know that's a pretty touchy subject around here."

So I trudged from Blind Ray Hynde's office and up to the Dean's office where the receptionist ducked behind her counter.

"Where'd you go?" I said.

"I don't want to appear complicit," said the receptionist's voice.

I looked around, but suddenly there was no one everywhere.

"Just go knock on his door," said the small voice.

I walked through the office of empty desks like a gunslinger. It was quiet. Too quiet. Almost completely quiet but for the thrumping of a hundred hearts behind the desks. I found the Dean's door. Dean Egg, Society of Jesus. The door opened a crack and the Dean peered out. "Oh," whispered the Dean. "Ooohh, ooohh."

"Blind Ray Hynde said you wanted to see me," I said.

"No, not really," said the Dean very softly.

Through the crack the Dean looked very much like a thin egg, almost as tall as me, frail and pale, his thin white fingers held his pale forehead; he wore black with a priest's collar.

"Maybe you could just go away," whispered the Dean.

"Then what?" I said.

"Then I'll fire you?" the Dean said.

"Can I come in?" I asked.

"I don't think that would be advisable," said the Dean. "It would violate our policy of cultural tolerance."

"You can't be tolerant?"

"Not of intolerant people."

"Isn't there implicit disapprobation in tolerance?" I said. "You only have to tolerate something you don't like."

"All opinions are tolerated here but the wrong ones," the Dean squeaked.

"I suddenly have intolerable opinions," I said.

"You support slavery," said the Dean. "You've been hiding it for decades."

"Only in the context that I work for almost nothing," I said.

"Well, there you have it," said the Dean. "Then being fired shouldn't affect your lifestyle. Think of your loyalty to the University. We won't be sued and we can hire somebody fresh out of grad school for half what we pay you."

"I was trying to be funny," I said.

"Maybe that's your problem," the Dean whispered. "I like you, Professor Shark. I just have to despise what you do."

"Teach?"

"Please, don't make me," said the Dean.

"Some n-word," I said.

"Oh, ooohh," said the Dean. He quivered. His knees buckled.

"I'm sorry," I said.

"You are?"

"Yes," I said. "Does that make it better?"

"Yes. You've admitted your guilt," said the Dean. "Thank you, Professor Shark. I thank you on behalf of the whole University community. And I appreciate your decades of hard work and dedication. You're fired."

"I'm not fired," I said.

"You're not?"

"No."

"You admitted your guilt."

"I said I was sorry," I said.

"Sorry for what?" said the Dean.

"I don't know," I said. "You tell me."

"If you're sorry, you must be sorry for something," said Dean Egg. "That's logic."

"Aren't there procedures for this?"

"These are the procedures," said the Dean. "Patricia came here and wept. Her husband wept. Her daughter wept. There was a lot of weeping. Ray Hynde cried. I cried, too. These are horrible accusations."

"Did they mention Thanksgiving?"

"That's why it's so shocking," said the Dean. "To all of us."

"I'm getting a lawyer," I said.

"Oh!" said Dean Egg as he collapsed to the floor. "Oh!"

The La-La Holyan

LA-LA HOLY ENGLISH PROFESSOR USES N-WORD IN CLASS

Professes To Prefer Racism To Catholicism
Seeks to Abolish the Emancipation Proclamation

When I staggered home, Diosa handed me a shot of rye and a beer.

"You really blew it this time," she said.

"So divorce me," I said.

"And pay alimony? Fat chance."

"It must have been something I said," I said.

Mervyn Delamore called me. He still taught a class at La-La Holy and flew down once a week in his private jet. "Patricia D'Aneesha was in my office crying," Mervyn said.

"She should cry in my office," I said. "That might get us somewhere."

"I think she feels you're circling the wagons, so to speak," said Mervyn.

"Because she's on the warpath," I said.

"Don't mix your racist metaphors with me, buster," said Mervyn. "I cover a lot of bases."

"Without basis," I said.

"You got it. I don't mean to condescend, Señor Tiburon," said Mervyn, "but you can't call somebody the N-word."

"Do you think I called Patricia the N-word?" I said.

"You called me a fairy."

"Did you go to the Dean?"

"You're lucky I didn't."

"You can't be a fairy here, Mervyn. Catholic school, it's don't ask, don't tell."

"Only because they're all in the closet."

"Does Patricia really think I called her an N-word?" I said.

"She doesn't know for sure," said Mervyn. "She wasn't paying attention."

"Did she mention Thanksgiving?"

"She was napping and woke up when you said it," Mervyn said. "At that moment she realized that everything you do is a charade which hides your true feelings of racism, and she realized her place in this racist culture which, like you, still believes in slavery."

"Mervyn. Remember last month, when I went up top Santa Rosa and helped you campaign for the Ewok gambling casino?"

"Miwok," said Mervyn. "How many other people of color do you have in there?"

"Living ones? I don't know," I said. "I'll have to check."

"Well you better."

"Does Japanese count?"

"No," said Mervyn.

"Philippino?"

"Don't get smart with me. Jews and Italians have picked up some ethnic weight recently, wop, kike, those words are out."

"The Irish are hot," I said.

"Only dancing and singing girls," Mervyn said.

"Not poets?"

"Irish poets have been around forever. Nobody cares."

"I better find out what I said in there," I said. .

"No kidding," said Mervyn. "She'll talk to me. I'll work as a double agent."

"That's great," I said.

"Don't be cynical, Señor Tiburon. You're in big trouble. But look at it this way, at least you've chased her out of the wood pile."

"It's hard for me to look at it that way," I said.

"That's because I can say it and you can't," said Mervyn.

I put down the phone.

"Father," said Jesus, "did you fuck up again because of your autism?"

"I'm afraid he did," Diosa said.

"Will you lose your job?" Jesus asked.

"I don't know," I said.

"That would really affect my lifestyle," Jesus said.

"I suppose you don't have any miracles up your sleeve," I said.

"I'm saving them for the Battle of the Bands," said Jesus.

"Have a drink, Shark," said Diosa. She'd been downstairs. She handed me a bourbon on the rocks.

"Maybe I'm a racist," I said.

"And I'm a kangaroo," said Diosa.

"Maybe you're a kangaroo," I said.

Anyway, I showed up for fiction writing seminar.

"Where's Patricia?" said Ari Kardashian.

"She was in here?" I said. "Could I speak to the registered students in private?"

Three people stood up from the sea of the dead and followed me out of the room. One of them was Ari who was Armenian and had been to Armenia twice, was marrying an Armenian physician and had connections to the Armenian Mafia. He liked to write about Armenia.

"I'm in trouble," I said.

"Something you said, I bet," said Brain McDonald. Brain was kind of old for a student, probably as old as my father.

"Aren't you a little old, Brain?" I said.

"I'm registered," said Brain. "If that's the dividing line."

"If you were going to get in trouble, you should have just had sex with me," said Rhonda Riordon. "In fact," Rhonda Riordon added, "now that you're in trouble already, isn't that like a *reductio ad absurdum*? Doesn't that mean you can do whatever you want now?"

"A little knowledge is a dangerous thing," I said.

"You quoted from *Blazing Saddles*," said Ari.

"*Blazing Saddles*?" I said.

"You were talking about my story," Ari said.

"My story," said Rhonda Riordon.

"I thought it was my story," said Brain, "though I don't remember anything about *Blazing Saddles*."

"Wait!" said Peter Alaska, emerging from the classroom. "I forgot I was in the class!"

"Are you registered?" said Brain. "That's the dividing line."

"I think writing a check is the dividing line," I said.

"I never thought of it that way," said Brain.

"That could be construed as anti-Jesuit," Ari said.

"Professor Shark is eccentric," said Rhonda Riordon. "An eccentric part of the La-La Holy community."

"My God," said Peter, who had a sweeping, dark widow's peak, a jutting jaw and an ax-handle nose. He looked Romanian, he looked like a vampire, but he was Greek. "Writing the check, my God," said Peter.

"It's those kinds of comments that get you in trouble," Ari said to me. He used to work at MGM where he did nothing. Everyone else in his department at MGM, people who did things, made mistakes and lost their jobs, but Ari survived two regime changes without even knowing what his department was or what it did. After seven years he ran into me at a party and I convinced him to quit his lucrative, easy job at MGM to pursue a worthless Master's Degree at La-La Holy. Here at La-La Holy, Ari no longer did nothing, but did everything.

Unbeknownst to almost everyone, Ari was running La-La Holy on his laptop. It was hard work and the pay was lousy. He had no medical insurance and was experiencing some pain in his kidney that was about to almost kill him.

"It was my story," said Peter.

"It wasn't Patricia's story?" I said.

"Patricia was sleeping," Ari said.

"But she sure woke up when you said the N-word!" Peter Alaska said.

Later that night, Ari brought me to his office and his laptop computer from which he ran everything.

"Ever been to Italy?" said Ari.

"Yes," I said.

"In every church, a camera on every painting. A priest in a back room sitting in front of fifty TV's."

"I've seen it," I said. "God isn't as omniscient as he used to be."

"The Lord helps those who help themselves," Ari said. "Here at La-La Holy, a crucifix in every classroom. A microphone and video camera in every one of them."

"So somebody's got the goods," I said.

"Me," said Ari.

He turned on the screen of his laptop. I was discussing Ari's story. In Ari's story, an Armenian liberation militia had taken over a Russian Soviet armory. The main character held a gun on twenty Russian soldiers while his compatriots hightailed it with the stolen weaponry, but now that his comrades had fled, it seemed he was badly outnumbered. Meanwhile, back in the class, Patricia was asleep to my right. "I hadn't thought the situation out well enough," said Ari in the video. "I don't know what to do."

"He should take *himself* hostage," said Rhonda Riordon, "and leave."

"Ha! That's absurd!" I said. "Like in *Blazing Saddles*. But there it's comedic. I'm quoting here, of course." Then I put my arm around my own throat and held my index finger to my head and said, "Nobody take a step closer or I'll shoot the n—!"

Patricia woke up and blinked twice.

"So I'm exonerated," I said.

"Hardly," said Ari.

"They've got it on tape. I quoted the black sheriff. The movie's on TV all the time."

"You think they're going to admit they've got cameras in the crucifixes?"

"I'll take one down," I said.

"And die a miraculously convenient death by electrocution."

"The Jesuits?"

"Remember Caron Honor's death?"

"The basketball player?" I said. "The Jesuits were involved?"

"That team was on the verge of a major coke scandal," Ari said.

"Dean Egg?" I said.

"A clueless pawn," said Ari Kardashian. "But ruthless."

"Well I have witnesses," I said.

"They're white or unregistered," said Ari. "Besides, it would violate Patricia's right to privacy."

"Where are the unregsistered people on that video?" I said.

"For all practical purposes, ghosts. They don't show up on video. It's a bane of paranormal research."

"What about my right to privacy," I said. "What about academic freedom."

"You're free to say anything you want and they're free to fire you. It's your word against hers now anyway," said Ari. "I've seen this go down at MGM. Your odds aren't good. But they don't want this getting outside the school, either."

"So if they fire me I might talk."

"You got it," said Ari. "That would be bad for them. Get a lawyer. Lie low. Build a defense. Don't admit guilt, but don't do anything untoward or they might take you out. In the meantime, I'll see what I can do from the inside. And if I get you out of this," said Ari Kardashian, "I'll want an A in that class."

So I called my old friend, Bob, who got rich prosecuting for the people against Union Carbide in Bopal. As you might remember, Bob was my old horse buddy when he used to live almost next door in Topanga on a twenty-four acre ranch. Bob introduced me to my horse, Jackie O, and at first I kept Jackie O right there at Bob's place. For two years or more Bob and I met every morning at dawn and rode together. Likely, without Bob, Jackie O might have killed me, if only by accident, though Bob, who liked to buy and sell horses, spent all his time trying to convince me to sell Jackie O before she killed me and, of course, I didn't listen to him and she almost killed me a lot of times. It was love.

Bob ran the American Oceans Campaign with Ted Danson. For a little while, Bob and his wife, Connie Mississippi, a wood sculptor, were me and Diosa's best friends. They didn't eat meat or raw vegetables; they didn't drink alcohol and they farted a lot. They were both Diosa's height, if much shorter than her per capita. Bob and Connie always told me that I was blocking my bounty. I had a bounty block. Writer's block, never, but bounty block in abundance. It was my own damn fault I was neither rich nor successful. Write better, said Bob. I said, I'm writing as good as I can!

One day out of nowhere Bob and Connie picked up and moved to Santa Fe where Connie went in and out of retirement from wood sculpting like a wood sculpting Sugar Ray Leonard and Bob was making a fortune selling water for the Apaches to the state of New Mexico and taking a percentage on both ends.

Bob was my friend and a lawyer, too, so I called him.

"Hey buddy," said Bob.

"Hey Bob," I said.

"How's your property dispute?"

"Ongoing," I said.

"Have you sold your horse?" said Bob.

"No," I said. "Listen Bob," I said, and told him abnout my current predicament at the University of La-La Holy.

"Quit and move here," said Bob.

"I don't have a job out there," I said.

"Pretty soon you won't have a job there," Bob said.

"What can I do?"

"You need to ask yourself why you'd want to be falsely accused of being a racist," said Bob.

"Maybe I am a racist," I said. "Unbeknownst to myself. Isn't that the pattern?"

"No, no," said Bob. "It's way deeper than that. You're obviously not a racist. Maybe you're telling yourself you don't want to teach there anymore."

"No one wants to teach there anymore," I said.

"And how many teachers are being accused of racism? Probably everyone else there is racist and this is some kind of mass transference."

"That's not what transference is," I said.

"Either way, it's happening," said Bob. "Boy, I really feel sorry for you."

"Shark!" said Wil Deeth when I called. Wil had become the Chief Executive for the County of Los Angeles Sheriff's Department. He was in charge of certifying all the lawyers in the most populous, litigious county in America. "I was hoping not to hear from you," said Wil.

"You and whose army?" I said.

"I've heard you were becoming difficult," Wil Deeth said.

"I'm becoming ineffable," I said.

"You wouldn't want to explain that," said Wil.

"And ephemeral," I said. "And macabre."

"Why do I get the feeling I'm becoming an exercise in arcane dialogue?" Wil Deeth said.

"Would it have something to do with the level of conversation?" I said.

"Shark," said Wil, "I can't help you. I'd love to help you but I can't."

"You're the most powerful lawyer in the County of Los Angeles," I said.

"That's why I can't help you," said Wil. "I'm too powerful."

"You owe me for getting you your B.A. You're the lawyer son I never conceived."

"So it would be a conflict of interest," said Wil.

"Anything you do would be a conflict of interest," I said.

"That's why this is such a great job," Wil said. "I can't ever do anything."

"Advice?" I said.

"I'd really back off that re-instituting slavery stuff," Wil said.

"I quoted *Blazing Saddles*," I said. I had to explain the whole thing again. "Patricia was sleeping."

"Maybe you should hire a lawyer," said Wil.

"There's a video and there are witnesses."

"A black female lawyer would be your best bet," Wil said. "It will cost you a fortune, but you have to weigh it against getting fired and having your reputation permanently ruined."

"This is Kafkaesque," I said.

"Kafka," said Wil. "What would you recommend I look at?"

It was at this time that the Coven of Canvas-Hatted Witches were attacking my house with picks, axes, shovels, and invectives. And I'd just received an e-mail about my old friend, Russ Schneider's, suicide. He'd been a writer, of course. A deadly Santa Anna wind swept the land and huge wildfires raged across Southern California, the closest only ten miles north, swept across the mountains for thirty miles, from Ventura to the border of

Glendale. Some Topangans were comforted by the fact that Chatsworth, Canoga Park, and Woodland Hills sat between Topanga Canyon and the fire, but a shift in the wind could take it into the forested Santa Susana Mountains, into Calabasas, and down into Malibu or Old Canyon. If you knew the wind and the terrain, you knew this.

At sunset, I stood on my top deck, under the smoken sky, in the hot, still air. Below me the coven hacked at my foundation and above me the sky filled with red smoke, the murky sun weeping blood, and now, from the air, the ashes fell in the shape of leaves. They coated my hands, my head, my house, my remaining deck, falling, still warm, silently falling, red embers of the fire, ashen breath of trees, the graying ground under the red sky, the ashes fell, fell silently and silently fell, fell upon the living and the dead.

I went inside and found Diosa masturbating behind the newspaper while doing the crossword.

"Thinking of me?" I said.

"Of course, my love," said Diosa. Though she was really thinking of Barak Obama.

"Let's go for a ride," I said.

We hopped into her white 4-Runner and headed for Topanga State Beach. We walked on the shore, the ocean flat and pink under the ashen off-shore wind. I looked out at the sea. "I'm sorry," I said to the air, "I've been preoccupied."

"So pray for rain," Diosa said.

It's complicated, but in the right circumstances, like before a storm, I can make it rain.

Diosa and I sat and watched the quiet sea. Then we got back in the car, drove up the coast and trekked down the cliffs to the State Beach at El Matador. Dusk fell. The smoke thickened, then filled with a breath of fog. In an hour it began to drizzle. We stood and I took Diosa's hand.

"Well, Shark" said Diosa, "at least you're good for something."

"Good for two things," I said. "Good for nothin' and good for shit." That was something my dad always said.

We got in the car and drove back down to the Boulevard. It was raining steadily now. I turned up the canyon. Then, around the first curve, the back of the Toyota fishtailed. I let up on the gas and the car went into a slide. I turned into it and waited for the vehicle to straighten out. It didn't. I drove straight into a telephone pole.

24 HOUR GRILL

WHEN I DROVE DIOSA'S CAR into the telephone pole I wasn't even drunk. But I had to talk to the Sheriff and the paramedics and then the California Highway Patrol. I had to spend a lot of time talking to the authorities with their faces really close to mine. If you've ever been arrested you know this routine.

"Been drinking?"

"No."

"Where were you?"

"The beach."

"Little cold and wet for the beach."

"It was dry when we got there?"

"What did you have to drink?"

"Nothing."

"How many did you have?"

"None."

"Where were you?"

It was a mistake not to just jump in the ambulance. I left a message for my insurance agent and called my insurance agency, called a tow truck to get the 4-runner towed. We got a ride home from the tow truck guy.

"People don't know how to drive in the rain," said the tow truck guy. He had a light blue shirt with white pin-stripes and a red oval on his pocket that said *Jose*, dark blue khakis, black work shoes.

"I know how to drive in the rain," I said.

"Sure," said Jose.

"It was like a hand reached out and threw us into the pole," Diosa said.

Out in the rain and dark I hadn't noticed, but the air bag had hit her in the face and chest and she was pretty cut up.

"You're hurt," I said.

"My ribs hurt," said Diosa.

So as soon as we got home I drove Diosa to the UCLA Med Center in Santa Monica. We waited in the emergency room, then a nurse led us inside and took Diosa's temperature and blood pressure. Diosa sat on the first table near the entrance. I remembered the room. A year ago she'd had an undetected ectopic pregnancy that ruptured. She lost a liter of blood and came within a few minutes of dying.

"Remember this room?" I said.

"No," said Diosa.

"You were on that last table on the other end."

"I was in pain," said Diosa. "I wanted to die."

"You lost a liter of blood," I said. "Your blood pressure was down to 40/20."

"You saved me, you bastard. I wanted to die."

"Then you fell in love with your surgeon," I said.

"So what? I always fall in love with my surgeon. I didn't fuck him."

"You would have," I said.

"Maybe," said Diosa. "I'm leaving you as soon as you get me through this."

Then a young, Asian doctor, Dr. Ming, came in and looked at Diosa, dabbing her facial cuts with a wet swab and touching her ribs. "Does that hurt?" said the doctor.

"Yes," Diosa said.

"You took quite a pop," said the doctor.

"Car accident," I said.

"You're going to have two black eyes," the doctor said to Diosa.

"Shit," Diosa said. "Will I need plastic surgery?"

"I doubt it. We'll x-ray you."

"Can I get a face lift?" said Diosa.

"So, where in the house were you when this happened?" said the doctor.

"Car accident," I said. "I drove into a pole."

"Were you fighting?"

"I drove into a pole," I said.

The doctor looked at Diosa.

"He drove into a pole," she said.

"Well we better get you x-rayed," said the doctor, and two chubby nurses, one black and one white, in pale green uniforms, put Diosa on a gurney.

"Remember when they wheeled you off for your emergency operation?" I said.

"No," said Diosa.

"I said I loved you and I'd be waiting for you."

"I wanted to die," Diosa said.

"You flipped me off," I said.

Then the two chubby nurses in pale green uniforms wheeled Diosa out of the emergency area and into the x-ray room where the nurses told her it would be okay if she told them why I hit her.

"Even if he didn't?" said Diosa.

"Even if he did," said the black nurse. Her tag said Jolanda.

"He drove into a pole," Diosa said.

"How did he do that?" said the white nurse named Barbara.

"Very slowly," said Diosa.

"You're pretty banged up," said Barbara.

"It was a big, hard, pole," Diosa said.

"You sure we're not speaking metaphorically here?" said Jolanda.

"I've never been hit that hard by metaphor," said Diosa. "By a poet maybe, but not a metaphor."

"Your old man a poet?" said Jolanda.

"Not even close," said Diosa.

"You can tell us if he hit you," said Barbara. "It's okay."

"For whom?" said Diosa.

"Has he hit you before?" said Barabara.

"He's never hit me," said Diosa.

"You saying he's not man enough to hit you?" said Jolanda.

"He drove into a pole," Diosa said.

In came the Pakistani x-ray technician, Rufus. "Is that your husband waiting for you?" he said.

"More or less," said Diosa.

"He's right-handed?" Rufus said.

"It depends what he's doing," said Diosa.

"Punching?"

"He drove into a pole," said Diosa.

"Were you wearing a seat belt?"

"Yes."

"The air bags deployed?"

"Yes," said Diosa.

"People get their ribs broken because they're covering their faces with their arms," said Rufus.

Anyway, it went on like that until they wheeled Diosa out of there.

"They think you hit me," Diosa said to me when we were alone.

"Just doing their job," I said.

"Why aren't they grilling you?" said Diosa. "You're the one who hit me."

"Because I'm scary," I said. "I hit people."

Dr. Ming came in and explained that x-rays were no longer processed on site and they'd have to wait to get the x-rays back from the big hospital in Westwood that was experiencing extremely heavy volume that night.

"Lots of car accidents," I said. "First rain."

"You're pretty defensive," said Dr. Ming.

"I drove into a pole!" I said.

"As you've insisted," said Ming.

"Can I please get something for the pain?" said Diosa.

Dr. Ming silently scrutinized me, then walked out.

"He thinks I hit you to get your pain medicine," I said.

"Maybe if you shaved once in a while," said Diosa.

Three hours later we were still waiting for the x-rays.

"Make them give me something for the pain," Diosa said to me.

"Right," I said. "Me."

"A real man would make them," said Diosa.

"They're making us wait here to see if we'll fight," I said.

"Maybe if you wore something besides Uggs and pajamas," said Diosa.

"I don't wear pajamas," I said.

"Not in bed," said Diosa.

"The next time I punch you I'll wear a suit," I said.

AT THE UNIVERSITY OF LA-LA HOLY: "A" FOR LACK OF EFFORT

I GOT AN EMAIL FROM Dean Egg. "Come to my office," it said. So I drove to the campus of the University of La-La Holy and walked through the cavern of empty desks leading to the Dean's door. I knocked. A pale effigy of shadow appeared behind the translucent glass.

"It's me," I said. "You said you wanted to see me."

"Oh," quivered Dean Egg's shadow, "not see you."

I waited silently while the Dean's white bones rattled on the other side of the door.

"Will you give Patricia an **A**, Professor Shark?" simpered Dean Egg.

"She's not in my class," I said.

"That's okay," said Dean Egg. "Give her an **A** and sign this."

A letter appeared under the door. It said that I called Patricia the N-word and I was sorry.

"I'll keep a copy for your file and give one to Patricia and then she says everything will be all right, she won't go to the news as long as you quit."

"She's already been to the news. The La-La Holyan," I said.

"No one reads the La-La Holyan," said the Dean. "Not the students, not the editors, not even the writers. It's why we give them absolute freedom."

"I quoted *Blazing Saddles*," I said. "You already know."

"No!" said Dean Egg.

"I didn't call her anything. She was sleeping."

Dean Egg held his ears. "You violated her comfort zone," said Dean Egg.

"I have it on video," I said. "You do, too."

"We have you on video stealing that video," Dean Egg said.

"I'll take early retirement with full salary and complete benefits," I said.

"I can offer you early retirement with no salary and no benefits," said the Dean.

"Just fire me," I said.

"Will you sue us?" quivered Dean Egg.

"Of course."

"We know about you beating your wife," Dean Egg whispered.

"I drove into a telephone pole," I said. .

"A racist and a wife beater," said the Dean. "I've always been a big supporter of you, Professor Shark, but there are those in the Jesuit Community who feel, well, threatened by your continued presence."

"You're threatening me," I said.

"We're the Jesuits," Dean Egg said. "We never threaten. We convince."

THE LIFE OF JESUS IN LOS ANGELES: JESUS CURES THE BLIND BOY

"JESUS," I SAID.

"Yes, Father," said Jesus.

"Mrs. Davenport called today."

"I hope all these phone calls are doing some good," Jesus said.

"She said your followers are claiming you cured a blind boy," I said.

"Oh, pshaw, Father," said Jesus.

"Some kids saw you rubbing your saliva on his eyes."

I parked my truck in the carport. Jesus turned to me. "If you hit somebody right between the shoulder blades, really hard, you can knock his contacts right out of his eyes. Some jocks did that to a nerd. I found his contacts and helped him put them back in."

"You couldn't find a water fountain?"

"You can't use the bathrooms, Father, someone will kill you. Besides, he is a boy, I am not."

"A little saliva then," I said.

"Indeed," said Jesus.

"Mrs. Davenport got the story wrong," I said.

"Misinformation travels fast," Jesus said.

"Maybe you need to get better control of your followers," I said.

"Really, Father. Control? Coming from you?"

"I'm sorry," I said.

"I am the daughter of God, and everybody else, all of them, are children of God. I'm going to go inside now and make myself a baloney sandwich," Jesus said.

THE BOOK OF CLEAVAGE

RHONDA RIORDON CAME to see me in my office. She wore a pale blue Danskin over a push-up bra, her large breasts bulging forward and together like pillows of flesh. Her white skirt fell softly, embroidered with lavender flowers, hemmed with lavender lace; it fell just above her knees. She wore white heels, patent leather, with the slightest lavender hue. Her black hair fell over her shoulders, her blue eyes steady under dark brows. Her lips suddenly looked more full. She sat down as I turned from my computer. Usually I avoided these kinds of encounters by closing my door and talking loudly to myself, but Rhonda was hip to the ruse. Rhonda crossed her beautiful legs.

"You're looking at my breasts," said Rhonda Riordon.

"No," I said. "I'm looking at your legs."

"Please don't look at my legs, Professor Shark," said Rhonda Riordon.

I raised my eyes to look Rhonda Riordon in her eyes, but I got stuck on her breasts.

"You're discriminating against me because of the way I look," Rhonda Riordon said.

"I'm not discriminating against you, I'm staring at your breasts," I said.

"Are you going to get mad and hit me?" said Rhonda Riordon. "Or do you just beat your wife?"

"Only my wife," I said.

"You're a fidelitist," said Rhonda Riordon. "You're discriminating against me because you're not married to me."

Rhonda Riordon had sure nailed this discrimination thing. "Rhonda," I said out of some deep, tired, absurd inclination that went against every rational impulse, to pull something teachable from the context, "if I turn around and pull my pants down and show you my naked butt, am I guilty for pulling my pants down or are you guilty for staring?"

Rhonda Riordon's breasts heaved. She began to sob. "There's a power differential," she coughed. "You're a man and a professor in a patriarchal hierarchy. I'm dressed like this to assert what little power I have over you."

I looked around my office at my six thousand books and my five hundred 1:40 scale rubber dinosaurs, determined, when I returned my gaze to Rhonda Riordon, to look her in the eyes. I failed. "Rhonda," I said to her heaving breasts, "you've gotten an education."

"Thanks to you," wept Rhonda Riordon. "I have no peers. Look at me. And now I'm intelligent and educated."

"You have to ask yourself, 'what next?'" I said.

"Okay," said Rhonda Riordon. "What's next?"

"*What* next," I said.

"You leave your wife?"

"This body would soon disappoint you," I said.

"You could use your tongue," Rhonda Riordon said. Rhonda Riordon uncrossed and re-crossed her slender legs. "Oh fate!" cried Rhonda Riordon. "To think it's all simply because you are my advisor because my name begins with R!"

THE GREAT ESCAPE:
DO NOT GO GENTLE

THERE WAS NOTHING LEFT to do but drive to Death Valley and celebrate me and Mingo's fiftieth birthdays. So we packed off with Jesus, Gabriela, Mingo, and their kids, Eva and Anahi and drove to Death Valley. It was great being with those guys because you could never feel tortured. Gabriela and Mingo didn't know how to drive yet, so I drove my new gray truck and Diosa drove her replacement car, a big white Ambassador we named The Ghost. I took us in the back way, from the south, on California Route 178. It was great. We didn't see anybody. The narrow road was blown over with sand.

"Are we lost?" Gabriela asked me.

"How could we be lost?" I said. "We're on the only road."

"That, to me, means lost," she said.

Diosa followed behind with Mingo and the three kids who listened to separate music players in the back seat. All around, the low, brown-blue desert, rocks, sand, nothing, enough nothing to fill you with nothing.

"Do you like this?" Diosa asked Mingo.

"I love it," Mingo said.

"He loves it," Diosa told me over her cell.

"How about you?"

"I hate it," Diosa said. "My skin is aging by the second."

"Mingo loves this," I told Gabriela.

"He is from La Boca," said Gabriela. "A city. He is fascinated by this ruthless nature."

"You're from a city."

"Bahia Blanca," said Gabriela. "A farm with lights."

When we got to Bad Water, the lowest point on the continent, it was the first and last time Gabriela left a vehicle in daylight to do anything but transfer to motels or the other vehicle, which was only twice fewer times than Diosa, who ventured out again at Zabriskie Point and Dante's View. At Bad Water, groups of German and French tourists stood, arms spread out like angels, like scarecrows, like Robin Williams. The flat alkaline pond, the bad water, sat in white and reflected the dry blue hills; the temperature was 113 degrees.

"You see," I said. "We found it."

"Found what?" said Diosa.

"You call this found. I call this lost," Gabriela said.

"Where are the kids?" said Mingo.

The kids were in the Ghost, air conditioning on, listening to tunes.

Me and Mingo took off on our own and drove the Twenty Mule Team Trail, a gulch of fragile, bright yellow canyons under the blue sky, a big, white moon above us. At dusk, when the temperature cooled to 100, we all walked on the sand dunes and at night we drank twenty-year-old wine from my basement. We sat in the motel parking lot of Stovepipe Wells and watched shooting stars.

"This is amazing," Mingo said.

"What is this preoccupation with nature?" said Gabriela.

"I'm never, ever coming back here," Diosa said.

"Feel that hot wind," I said.

"I can feel it coming up through my toilet," said Gabriela. "It's everywhere."

"When I turn fifty I'm going to Paris," said Diosa.

"I'm going with you," Gabriela said.

"Is this making you forget for a while?" Gabriela said to me.

"Only when I laugh," I said.

"Is that some American joke?"

"It's an Asperger's joke," said Diosa.

"This is amazing," said Mingo, who got up, stretched, and staggered into the desert.

"Is he safe?" said Gabriela.

"Safer than us. We could be hit by a car," I said. "He's probably just taking a pee."

"He doesn't pee outside," Gabriela said, "unless you taught him something."

Mingo stumbled back. "I found something."

"What?" said Diosa.

"I don't know. Something," said Mingo. "A hidden spring."

"Let's look!" Diosa said.

"Out there! In that nature?" said Gabriela.

"Come on," I said.

"Call the kids," said Diosa. "Let's go!"

We dragged the kids out of the air conditioning and everybody gathered in the parking lot, in the hot wind, and followed Mingo into the desert, across the sand, between the occasional stands of desert grass, until he stopped under a small Mexican palm.

"Listen," Mingo said.

A hiss, and a slight gurgling.

"Look!" said Diosa, and from under the palm a trickle of clear, cool water.

"What's going on?" said Eva."

"Mingo found water," said Jesus.

"A well. One of the Stovepipe Wells," Diosa said.

"An ancient spring," Mingo said.

"*Mi hombre*" said Gabriela. "You would have saved a whole colony of imperialist despoilers."

"Or better, Mormons," I said.

"He couldn't have done it without me," Jesus said.

I reached into the thick grass that surrounded the palm.

"Don't do that, Shark," said Diosa. "You can't see."

But I reached into the grass, found the spigot, and turned the water off.

"What?" said Gabriela.

"A water spigot," I said.

"No," said Diosa.

I reached in again and turned it on. Then I turned it off.

"It could still be a well," Diosa said to Gabriela.

"You mean the pipe it's connected to could be connected to a well," said Gabriela. "Do not feel bad, *mi flaco*," she said, patting Mingo's shoulder.

Mingo shrugged. "It changes nothing."

"Shark, destroyer of myth and beauty," Diosa said.

"It's why you all respect me," I said. "Even if you hate me for being a racist and wife beater."

"Fucker," said Diosa.

"Shark, are you a fucker?" asked Anahi.

"I'm afraid I am, Anahi," I said.

"A motherfucker?" said Anahi.

"Aniyi, *quieto*!" Gabriela said.

"It's a metaphor, Shark," said Diosa.

"Everything is, I suppose," I said.

"Yes, but this is a real fucking metaphor," said Gabriela.

We stood for a moment, a shooting star ran across the sky.

"Turn the spigot back on, Shark," said Diosa. And I did.

Jade Night
Scenes of mad love. Days laid down like rags around our feet.
I stood with Motherwell, looking at the ruin of ruins in Mexico.
A fountain in the middle of the room. Nothing in the world
but rain. Nothing in the world but rain and rags and our two beings
rotating, totally washed. And this was the real place. Rub it.
Rub it till it tears you apart.
— Diosa

"Slow down!" screamed Gabriela.

"I'm going pretty slow," I said.

"This is amazing," said Mingo. He sat in the center of the club cab.

"Watch the road!" said Gabriela.

"I'm looking out for Diosa," who was following us out California 190 and over the Panamint Range. I'd never been on this road. I didn't expect it to be so spectacular: high, narrow ridges, sweeping moonscapes into deep, windswept valleys, airfull precipices. "She gets dizzy in these situations," I said.

"It's pretty amazing," said Mingo.

"Dizzy?" said Gabriela. "Dizzy? My children are in that car."

"Do you want to drive?" I said.

"Drive what? No. Isn't there another way out?"

"The way we came in. We'd have to turn around."

"Where are you going to turn around? You can't even fit one car on this pathway."

"I didn't expect it to be this amazing," Mingo said.

"Me either," I said.

"Will you watch the fucking road?" said Gabriela. "Don't look at the scenery. Drive. It is our job to look at the scenery and your job to drive."

"You're not looking at the scenery," I said.

"But I don't have to do my job. You have to do your job."

"I'm doing my job," I said.

"Don't look at me when you talk. Watch the road."

"What is the name of this place?" said Mingo.

"Death Valley," I said.

"No," said Mingo. "This specific place where we are at. Probably the Devil's something or other."

"Everything in this place is the Devil's something or other, Hell's something or other, Satan's something or other," Gabriela said.

"Whatever it is called, it is pretty amazing," said Mingo. "I did not expect it to be so amazing."

"I guess she's doing okay back there or she'd signal us," I said. "You don't want to stop and look around, do you?"

"It would be okay with me," Mingo said.

"No," said Gabriela. "Just drive. Watch the road, not the scenery. Drive. I do not want to stop on the Devil's Pathway. I want to leave Death Valley, never to return."

We wound up and up, still higher. Gabriela put her hands over her eyes. I checked the rear view mirror. Diosa was still following. We glided to the very top of the range where the mountainside fell away and briefly, for a bitter-sweet moment, there was only the expanse of never-ending sky. Then we wove back down, down, down into the plains, across the dry lake bed of Dry Lake Owens, into the sheer granite snowy edges of the Sierras and US Route 395. We stopped in Olancha, population 6, at a funky little Snack n' Gas store with mechanical gas pumps. Next store was a restaurant that was boarded up. Eva and Anahi raced around like electrons, wasting dollars, buying pop and chips and nuts and candy. A hot wind blew. Gabriela opened the truck door, felt the wind, closed the truck door. "The Devil's grocery store," she said.

"That was pretty amazing," Mingo said to Diosa. "Did you see much of it?"

"Much of what?" said Diosa.

"The scenery," I said.

"What scenery?" Diosa said.

We crossed above LA on Route 14 and stopped at Vasquez Rocks where every space movie ever made by Hollywood has been shot.

"Why are we here?" said Gabriela.

"I needed to get off the planet," I said.

"Now I understand this whole trip," said Gabriela. "You have star captain syndrome."

"To boldly go," said Mingo.

"Go boldly," I said.

"Into that good night," said Diosa.

Burn, burn against the dying of the light.

A LITERARY AGENT IN LOS ANGELES?
THE BIRTH OF MAGIC JOURNALISM

DEEP IN THE RECESSES of my many souls grew a desire to communicate to an audience larger than myself. Of course, this was artistic death, but death is inevitable and I had at least one artistic soul to give. Everything was happening at once. An actor, Paul Lieber, who'd come to one of my readings, optioned my horrid little memoir for a movie. He offered me no money whatsoever, which was right up my alley, or down my alley, one of those.

"Why?" I said.

"Because it's terrific. It's moving. It's universal."

"You talking about my memoir?"

"It would make a great movie," said Lieber.

"Because it's terrific? Anyway, I already have a movie about me."

"Do you want to write the screenplay?" said Paul Lieber.

"I wrote the book," I said.

"Yes," said Lieber, "but we'll need to shop a screenplay. Don't you want some control?"

"I don't think a screenplay can be controlled," I said.

"That might be true," Lieber said. "So, do you want to write it?"

"No," I said.

Boy, was I glad that was over.

A week later Lieber called me. I had been riding my sweet little horse

Jackie O when, back at my truck, I noticed that I had a message on my cell phone. "Hello, Shark," said the message, "this is Paul. I finished the screenplay. I worked really hard on it. Do you want to see it?"

I told him, no, but Paul Lieber sent me the screenplay anyway. I sat in my reading chair drinking Monopolowa potato vodka on the rocks and read it. Diosa sat across from me on the couch, watching a crime show with lots of bloody forensics.

"I could have been a forensic expert," said Diosa.

"A lawyer," I said. "Then I wouldn't need my lawyers to not do anything anymore."

"A doctor anyway," said Diosa. "I like blood."

I lifted the screenplay. "See this," I said. "Fame and fortune."

"Again," said Diosa.

"It's a little early," I said. "My spiritual guardian said sixty, like Gertrude Stein."

"Your spiritual guardian."

"I've been keeping him a secret for moments like this."

"Gertrude Stein told lies about her famous friends," said Diosa. "You just tell lies."

"She was born in Pittsburgh," I said.

"You weren't born in Pittsburgh," Diosa said. "You were born in Erie."

"But most people tell lies with some intention of telling the truth," I said, "even if it's delusional rationalization."

In fact, pardon the pun, this was something I'd been working on. Creative nonfiction was driving me crazy; true stories, stories based on true stories, fiction techniques to recreate the irreproducible facts because facts don't tell the truth, because the truth didn't tell the truth; it was driving me crazy! And exclamation points! Boy did I hate exclamation points! And so did Gertrude Stein!

So, "I'm inventing a new genre," I said. "Creative nonpoetry."

"Write when you get work," Diosa said.

Anyway, famous people were going to look at the screenplay, Paul Lieber said. Viggo Mortenson. David Duchovny. Nicholas Cage. Sundance. Lion's Gate. Producers with major studios. But if I was going to be famous, I needed a "How to Write" book waiting in the wings to exploit my fame. And I wouldn't just write another stupid laying down the birds book, bone by bone, I'd write an Anti-How-to-Write Book. And boy was it going to be funny. I wrote up an outline of my Anti-How-to-Write Book. I wrote an introduction. I wrote a few chapters. I read them to my graduate writing class. "Jesus Christ!" said my graduate students, obviously lying in their teeth. "This is great! This is what writers need to hear!"

"Because it's the truth!" I said. "It's the 21st Century! Everything is in decay! The writing world is blithering in market formulas! The time has come!"

"What are you, crazy?" said Diosa. "Did you get off your meds?"

In fact, I had got off my meds. My sweet little shrink had decided that my memoir caused Post Traumatic Stress Syndrome. Now, with this N-word thing, I needed meds. Meds! Meds!

"Boy," said Diosa, "I just figured you had Asperger's."

I liked Lexapro because it made me a chemical Buddha, but it also made me detached from my hard-ons.

"I get hard-ons, but I don't seem to care about them," I said to my sweet little shrink.

"You're lucky," said my sweet little shrink. "Some people don't even get hard-ons."

"So I'm fucked if I do," I said.

"And fucked if you don't," said my little shrink.

After that, very quietly and without telling anyone, I slowly weaned myself from the Lexapro. I started getting really big hard-ons that I cared about a lot. And really big ideas!

So, "What are you, crazy? Did you get off your meds?" Diosa said.

And I said, "Have you noticed these big fat hard-ons?"

"Fuckin' A," said Diosa.

"So I'm crazy, but I get big fat hard-ons," I said.

"You're really complex," Diosa said. "I never realized. When I first met you, I only noticed the hard-ons."

"That was a while ago," I said.

"It took me a while to get past the hard-ons," said Diosa. "But you were smart. That's what else."

"Really?" I said.

"Not really," said Diosa.

One thing about talking to Diosa, you didn't have to care about the result of the conversation. She was an anarchist and a surrealist to the bone. So I called up a new part-time colleague at La-La Holy, Phil Filson, who kept asking me to come over for dinner. Ironically, he ran a little magazine called *Real People Stories! (RPS!)*. He wanted a full-time job at the U of La-La Holy. Phil said he'd written a best seller about giving up being a gangster and finding God.

"My wife is a literary agent," said Phil. "She's getting me a movie deal."

"I'm having a movie," I said. "I could use a movie deal."

"My wife already has a movie deal," said Phil, "for a best seller she wrote under a pseudonym."

"It's that easy," I said.

"It's that easy," said Phil.

"We'll be dealing in movies!" I said.

"She's a literary agent with William Morris in New York!" said Phil.

"And she sells movies?"

"She can sell anything."

"Can she sell my Anti-How-to-Write Book?" I said. "It's smart and funny!"

"That's great!" said Phil. "Come over for dinner at my place. Bring Diosa. My wife loves to cook dinner!"

"Don't do it," said Diosa. "I knew them when they were poets."

Did I listen to her? Two weeks later me and Diosa drove to Phil's condo near the beach in Hermosa Beach. It was hard to find parking. There was a waning gibbous moon. And fog.

"Hey," said Phil and brought us in. We sat around a coffee table for an hour and a half while Phil's wife, Anna Fidel, fussed in the kitchen.

"You need help?" said Diosa.

"She doesn't need help," said Phil.

We drank water. We talked for another half hour, then Anna came out of the kitchen and said, "I decided to order out for Thai food."

"Great!" said Phil. He was writing another best seller! He was running on the beach! He was meditating at dawn!

An hour later the Thai food came and Anna caught it at the door. She took it into the kitchen. Phil went to the bathroom.

"Do I smell bad?" I asked Diosa.

"You stink of ambition," Diosa said.

"This water sure is good!" I said.

"He's getting skinny. She's put on weight. This marriage is on the rocks," Diosa said.

Phil came back. In an hour Anna emerged from the kitchen with a tray of aluminum containers full of tepid Thai food. "Boy, this was hard to put together," Anna said. The Thai food was okay. But it's LA. There are more Thais here than in Phucket.

"Boy, this is great!" said Phil.

"I'm writing another best seller," Anna said. "Under a pseudonym. Not because it's not any good. It's good. I already sold it."

"You're good at selling stuff," I said.

"Boy, she sure is!" said Phil.

"Did you look at my book?" I said.

"Five or six pages," said Anna.

"That's almost the whole introduction!" I exclaimed.

Nobody said anything for a while, so I said, "There are four chapters after the introduction, and there's an outline."

Anna got up abruptly and left the room. We sat there with Phil.

"This is sure fun," said Phil.

In a half hour Anna came back and sat down.

"What did you think?"

Anna got up again. Then she looked around the room, then turned and looked down at me. "You know, people who read how-to-write books don't want to know *how* to write. You seem to be writing for people who want to know how to write. I'm not sure there's a general audience for that."

"How about a specific audience who wants to know how to write?" I said.

"It's smart and uses arguments," said Anna.

"They're funny arguments," I said. "It's an Anti-How-to-Write Book!"

"Email me. I'll send you some material on how to write a proposal," said Anna.

"Will it be for someone who wants to know how to write a proposal?" I said.

"It's awful late," said Phil. It was almost nine.

Soon me and Diosa were outside in the fog, the fuzzy, waning glob moon smothering toward the horizon. We wandered toward Diosa's car.

"The moon is a metaphor of my life," I said.

"Don't be tedious," said Diosa.

But the moon on the horizon began to grow. It suddenly waxed. Expanded. The sky exploded with light. And then, just as suddenly, it waned, it faded behind the clouds.

"Metaphor," I said.

Diosa lit a cigarette. "I need a fucking drink," she said.

"I can't wait to get that proposal!" I said. If I hadn't used an exclamation point, Diosa might have believed me.

THE GODDESS DIES, NIGHTLY

I FOUND DIOSA ON THE COUCH doing a cross word puzzle. I knelt before her, lifted her skirt, and kissed her panties. I moved them aside and licked her until the two of us began to float. We floated near the ceiling. Then she placed me inside her and we rocked in the ecstasy of the air. Felt normal to me.

"You think you're so fucking special," Diosa said.

"I don't," I said.

"You do."

"We fly when we make love," I said.

Diosa said, "I do that for everybody."

> How you raised your middle finger in the air on the day
> I saved your life and how you held the baby
> in your arms like she were lead; how you moved inside
> yourself and wept; where do you go in there?
> why not keep something of yourself out here
> with us? Tears like bones. Tears like feathers.
> Tears as rust. I didn't want you to leave like that, with
> God all muddy on your shoes, wearing
> the ashes of all the dead; like snow on fire; palm

trees, swimming pools, shooting stars across
your breasts; captured birds; give them liberty, you said,
and give them nests.

"Give them desks,'" Diosa said.
"And apartments of their own," I said. "Virginia Woolf."
"I'm getting too predictable," Diosa said.

THE LIFE OF JESUS IN LOS ANGELES: JESUS RAISES THE DEAD

"MR. SHARK?" said Mrs. Davenport over the phone.

"Yes," I said.

"The father of Jesus?"

"Do I have to answer that?" I said.

"Your daughter is on the phone with us," said Mrs. Davenport. "She brought a boy back from dead," Mrs. Davenport said.

"What a rotten thing to do," I said. "Are you going to expel her?"

"Oh father," said Jesus. "It was just my buddy, Jared."

"The heroin addict," I said.

"He was dead," said Mrs. Davenport.

"He wasn't dead," Jesus said.

"The paramedics said he was dead," said Mrs. Davenport.

"CPR," said Jesus.

"She kissed him and he came back to life," said Mrs. Davenport.

"I love him," said Jesus. "I love him. Hell, I love everybody."

"You cannot kiss dead people on school grounds," said Mrs. Davenport.

"Jesus," I said, "was Jared dead?"

"Father, how can you ask that?" said Jesus. "You, of all people."

"Other students are calling her the Son of God," Mrs. Davenport said.

"Daughter of God," said Jesus, "and all of you are children of God."

"We cannot have God in our public schools!" said Mrs. Davenport.

"I really don't think we're going to solve this over the phone right now," I said.

"This is an administrative nightmare!" Mrs. Davenport said.

And lo, it came to pass that Jesus left high school and came to the University of La-La Holy. It was that easy.

THE XMAS PARTY

DIOSA AND I GOT READY to go to the University of La-La Holy
English Department Xmas party. I really hated the La-La Holy English
Department Xmas party and this year I was really going to hate it because
everybody would be side-stepping the rumors that I was a racist and a wife
beater. Food was ordered from the Mormon Marriot Corp. that ran La-
La Holy's food service and bookstore and the leftovers from the last seven
Jesuit receptions would be served up luke-cool to the ravenous faculty who
fell on it like a flock of realtors; cheap beers from unknown countries along
with exotic wines from New York and Missouri were guzzled pedantically.
Everyone had to get along. I had to wear clothes.

We sat at our dining table upstairs, bolstering ourselves, sharing vodka
tonics, rye crisps and brie. Diosa wore a flowing, knee-length, lavender
chiffon skirt, a tight blouse showing cleavage, tall platforms with thick high-
heels. She was driving me crazy.

"Can we make love?" I said.

"No."

"You wouldn't have to move."

"I'd have to fly with a skirt on. Have another drink."

We sat.

"Do you hate them?" Diosa said.

"Only for who they are," I said.

We kind of liked to sit together without speaking; it was the answer to the perfect couple questions everyone always annoyingly asked us: How do you two stay together? We're not together. How do you keep from fighting? We don't talk about anything.

In the old days, back in Salt Lake City, we kept a gram or so of coke around and used it for these kinds of occasions—back then, the horrible poet potlucks; dueling poet chefs; dueling personal rejection letters from the *New Yorker*; I always brought potato chips, Diosa brought chicken livers wrapped in bacon—one snort up each nostril and off you go, ready to meet the whorl. Now when you did coke it was hard not to think about Columbia.

Diosa picked up the plates of crackers and cheese. I went to take a leak, then I heard her scream. She lay at the bottom of the stairs, face down on the tile. Blood pooled near her forehead. I went to her. She moaned, "Shark." She puked, then fainted. Above her right eye blood flowed heavily into a pool on the tile. Her skin was torn. I could see the white of her skull.

I wet a wash cloth, wrapped ice in it, applied it to the wound. She gained consciousness enough to hold it there herself while I carried her down the steps to the Ghost. I got her in, put the seat back so she could lie down. "Don't let me bleed on my car," she said. But the movement down the windy, Topanga Canyon curves made her puke again. She moaned, wept, said, "I'm going to pass out," and did.

By the time I got her to the emergency room in Santa Monica her cheek had swelled to the size of a baseball. I got an icepack from the attendant and, after filling out the forms, rested Diosa's head in my lap. I cell phoned Jesus.

"We're at the emergency room," I said. "Diosa."

"Again," Jesus said.

"Can you help?"

"Let me get there," Jesus said.

"I caught my heel on the last step," Diosa said to me.

"You saved the dishes," I said.

"I got you out of the Xmas party."

Jesus came. Diosa smiled then. Jesus touched her forehead and her cheek. "Poor Momma," she said.

When they finally brought Diosa in they sat her on the same table as the time I drove into the telephone pole and Diosa broke two ribs. The same nurses,

Jolanda and Barbara, eyed me suspiciously. The same doctor, Henry Ming, came in. "Let's see," he said, and Diosa brought the ice down from her face.

The wound on her forehead had already closed.

"Remarkable," said Ming.

"An hour ago you could see her skull," I said.

I looked at Jesus.

Ming looked at me.

"I'm right handed," I said.

Ming turned back to Diosa and touched her right cheek which had begun to swell more. She winced.

"How did you get here?" Ming said.

"I drove," I said.

"You weren't afraid he'd hit a pole?" Ming said to Diosa.

"He was the only game in town," Diosa said.

"You're going to have a shiner," said Ming. "We'll need x-rays."

"Do I get plastic surgery?" said Diosa.

You couldn't use cell phones in the emergency room, so when Ming left me I sent Jesus to the lobby to call the Departmental Secretary, Lola, and tell her we were going to miss the party.

"Fell. Right," said Lola.

Ming came out and spoke to Jesus.

"Does your father hit your mother?" he said to her.

"They're more complex than that," said Jesus.

"But does he hit her?"

"Only with ideas," Jesus said.

"Does he hurt her?" said Ming.

"Some of them are not very good ideas," said Jesus.

"Is he violent?"

"Silly. I'd say he's silly," Jesus said.

"You're saying it's psychological abuse," said Ming.

"I'd say this is psychological abuse," Jesus said.

Back inside, Barbara took Diosa to the x-ray room and Jolanda sat with me.

"Hit another telephone pole?" said Jolanda.

"She fell down the stairs," I said.

"You push her?"

"She caught her heel on the last step."

"Big step."

"Yes," I said. "And a hard floor."

"You ever think of getting some help?" said Jolanda.

"I'll take all the help I can get," I said.

"Can I look at your hands?" said Jolanda.

I put my hands out, palms up. Jolanda looked at them, flipped them over, felt my knuckles.

"You soft-handed types are the worst," she said.

Diosa sat in the x-ray room with Barbara and the x-ray technician, Arjuna.

"How long are you going to let this go on?" Arjuna said to her.

"Until I get plastic surgery," Diosa said.

"You're an intelligent woman," he said. "How do you put up with this?"

"I use my intellect," said Diosa.

Barbara lined her up at the x-ray panel. "Don't let him keep doing this to you," she said.

"Driving me to the emergency room?" said Diosa.

"Hurting you."

"Love hurts," Diosa said.

Then the three of us were back at the examination table waiting for the x-rays. Ming came out with a copy of a negative. "Broken cheek," he said.

"Do I get plastic surgery?" said Diosa.

"No," said Ming. "This could take a year to heal."

Diosa looked at Jesus.

"You wanted a miracle?" Jesus said.

I put my hand on Diosa's left shoulder. I stroked her with my thumb from her nape to her ear.

"He punched me," Diosa said to Ming. "He hits me all the time."

I waited a week to call her from jail.

"How's it going?" I said.

"I like it," said Diosa. "I'm getting more done. But nobody takes out the trash."

"Animals?" I asked.

"We have animals?"

"Dogs?"

"I feed them from the table," she said.

"Cats?" I said.

"There are mice," said Diosa.

"Plants?"

"What plants?"

We were quiet for a little while.

"I just wanted to see what would happen, Shark," she said.

Well, I knew that. That was the whole point of everything, wasn't it, to see what would happen?

"It's a good thing I don't believe in free will," I said.

"Getting a lot of thinking done, I see," said Diosa. "That's dangerous for everybody. I better get down there and clear this up."

Later, I liked walking around with Diosa with her face all black and blue. I got a lot of respectful looks from other men. Diosa held my biceps with both her hands as we walked. "My hero," she said.

THE LIFE OF JESUS IN LOS ANGELES: JESUS AMONG THE HAMBURGER SELLERS

AND IT CAME TO PASS that Jesus sat with her disciples on a lawn at the University of La-La Holy in front of a hamburger stand owned by the Marriot Corp. and her disciples pestered her for wisdom.

"Should I wear a coat and tie to my Chase interview?" asked one of her disciples.

"Lo, I say unto you, of course," said Jesus. "What are you, fucking nuts? For if they are to appear as if naked before you, then you must be clothed before them, for if the world were naked, what point fashion and fashion magazines?"

"But Jesus," said a Young Republican, seeking to trick her, "you say you are a Communist and yet wear jewelry and make-up and get your hair done in Beverly Hills."

"I believe everyone should have jewelry and make-up and get their hair done in Beverly Hills," Jesus said.

But as the day wore on her followers said unto her, "Yo, Jesus, we've been sitting here all afternoon in front of this hamburger barbecue and yet we have no hamburgers."

"Baloney," said Jesus, "you're all rich Catholics and have lots of money." Yet she went up to the hamburger sellers and said, "How about giving my disciples some hamburgers?"

"No fucking way," said a big white kid with short hair, a black golf shirt, and a Marriot tag that said, "Bob."

"Yet you have all these hamburgers," Jesus said.

"That's the whole point, isn't it?" said Bob.

Jesus turned to her disciples. "Let the hamburger eaters come unto me," she said. She looked to the sky and said, "Father," as the light broke suddenly upon her. Then she took out my MasterCard and bought everyone hamburgers, even Bob.

SOMETIMES SI! SOMETIMES NO!

I GOT A PHONE CALL from my ex-landlord, Peter Alsop, who was married to Ellen Geer. Ellen ran the kind of famous Theatricum Botanicum, an open air theater in the canyon that was started by her dad, Will Geer, back in the McCarthy Era to give blackballed Hollywood Communist bi-sexual artists a place to work. Woody Guthrie built a house on the property; it was all cement and had no windows. Will Geer was a notorious bisexual, drug abuser, and Communist and later played Grandpa Walton on *The Waltons*. In some universes we all end up where we belong. Now Ellen produced and directed mostly Shakespeare plays there, though occasionally something modern, like *Long Days Journey* or *The Ice Man Cometh*.

Peter Alsop was a child psychologist who believed you could solve everything one person at a time. He wrote moral/morale songs that taught children good things, like his big hit "Sometimes Si! Sometimes No! That's the Way That Life Goes," which was about saying "No" to drinking alcohol to solve your problems. It was a catchy tune and it's a good thing you can't hear it or you'd never get it out of your head. I wanted to know when you got to say "Si." "Some other time," said Peter.

For a while me and Diosa rented offices behind the Will Geer Theatricum Botanicum, on the mountaintop above Heaven (you remember, it's in my movie). Diosa seldom went up there. It was nice up there. Too nice. She had asthma and smoked cigarettes. She had health standards. I got a bow and arrows and meditated shooting cardboard boxes. After my truck got totaled twice on Drinko de Mayo I bought a Jeep and while I was driving down the canyon toward the ocean I got hit by a flying boulder. The Jeep got knocked on its side and slid down the opposite side of the road. If anybody'd been coming the other way I'd be dead. Maybe I am dead. The police and my insurance company blamed me.

I miraculously escaped uninjured (or dead), but two days later, in my office on the mountaintop above Heaven, my rib cage went into muscle spasms—of course I didn't bring my cell phone—and it took me three hours to walk back down the mountain. Ellen Geer had been rehearsing Macbeth down below on the stage and when I finally got all the way down there all the actors shook my hand. "That's some of the best bellowing I've ever heard," said Macbeth. My doctor gave me drugs that made me forget everything, including what was happening in front of my face.

Back then the coven of canvas-hatted witches were still carrying off my land and drawing narrower and narrower property lines around my house. My Argentinean handyman, George, took apart my kitchen and suddenly began building on the land around my home. The canvas-hatted witches hired Mayans to carry boulders from the hill, George hired Hondurans to drill wells for cold pools filled by underground streams. The witches brought in Guatemalans to lug dirt from the land in baskets, George brought in Mexicans and started throwing up Tuff Sheds. It was exactly the kind of circus that caused T.C. Boyle to write *The Tortilla Curtain*, fire all his Hispanic gardeners and housekeepers up there in the Santa Barbara hills where once ensconced Michael Jackson and Ronald Reagan, and begin doing all his own landscaping and housework, and that's why he stopped writing and hired a woman from Belize to do it for him; that's why the marked change in style during that period and the drop in sophomoric scatological imagery.

But my property had become a dance of fluidity and liquidity, a breaking down of the lines of property and class. Huge *asados* sprung up everywhere around my home, slabs of meat grilled on cut-in-half oil cans, Budweiser beer to beat the band. A mariachi park sprung up near the roadside and musicians came from as far away as Garibaldi Square in Mexico City, "Mi pistola y mi corazon!"

But like everything, that ended. Still, I managed to save a Tuff Shed on the hill behind what was left of my house, put a ladder against the retaining wall leading up to it and said to Diosa, "Your new office."

"I need stairs," said Diosa.

"Ay! Caramba!" I said.

This led to a conference outside my kitchen around the infamous Glass Table(!) with those Argentineans, Gabriela and Mingo.

"How do we start?" I said.

"With martinis!" said Mingo.

"Oysters!" said Diosa.

And lo, oysters and martinis appeared upon the table.

"Am I going to have big tits in this scene?" said Gabriela.

"If it were up to me," I said.

"It is up to you."

"He wants me to climb that little tiny ladder," said Diosa.

"I'm a cruel bastard," I said.

"Look at me, with these little tits," said Gabriela.

"You don't have little tits," said Mingo.

"My daughters have bigger tits and they are mere children," said Gabriela.

I always found it hard to keep up with Gabriela's children. One daughter got younger as the other grew older, another, by a previous marriage from before Gabriela was disappeared, lived in New Jersey and collected babies. "That girl, she loves babies," Gabriela said. Whenever these Argentineans showed up things got increasingly surreal.

Gabriela laid her huge breasts on the glass table. "That's better," she said.

"Now let's move on to the stairs," said Diosa. "Just give me some stairs."

"Tits are easier," I said.

We drank champagne, then moved on to Malbec, a baguette and cheese.

"We have nothing in this house but a glass table and you want stairs to your new office," I said.

"What about your horse," said Mingo.

"My horse doesn't live here."

"Yes, what about your sweet little horse?" said Gabriela.

"Think of the shoes I could buy for the cost of keeping up that horse," said Diosa.

"And stairs," said Mingo.

Diosa touched my hand. "You should have an office here, too," she said. Ah, the you too card.

Later, alone, after the women went to bed and I sat up with Mingo drinking bourbon and smoking pot and salvia, Mingo said to me, "I did it for you, my friend. They are good women. We are lucky." Which was complex Argentinean male advice about getting laid.

So the Glass Table Collective had clearly sided against me. I don't even know why I resisted, resistance was futile. I fired George and found a Tibetan carpenter named Gendin and traded my motorcycle to him for the stairs. Gendin also put my house back together in three days.

"Have you been to Bhutan?" I asked Gendin.

"Sure," said Gendin.

"The Tiger's Nest?" I asked him.

"Sure," Gendin said.

"Was it built by flying monks?" I said.

"Sure," Gendin said.

"Were you ever a flying monk?"

"Sure," said Gendin."

"I love you, Shark," said Diosa.

"You just love me for my stairs!" I said.

Diosa took a credit card and in a blink had a Tuff Shed placed on top of all the debris George had left in front of the house. I hired flying Mayan monks to carry all the stuff from the shacks on the mountaintop above Heaven down the mountain and then trucked the stuff over to my house and stuffed it into the new Tuff Sheds. Material reality was becoming dangerously cogent. Then the world's financial system collapsed. Whew!

Meanwhile, as usual, people were running for president. It was the most important presidential election in the history of the United States, if not the world, since the last one. Everything was at stake. The ice caps were melting, the economy smelting, there were two disastrous wars in Afghanistan and Iraq, India and China were sending space ships to the moon!

Then I got that phone call from Peter Alsop.

"Hey," said Peter, "you moved out."

"It transcended Heaven. We couldn't stands it no longer," I said. "We used flying monks."

"We need to get together immediately and figure out how to solve everything one person at a time," said Peter.

"I think it's going to have to be solved by a lot of people simultaneously," I said.

"That will never happen," said Peter Alsop.

So Peter got in his old beat up Mercury Montego Minivan and picked up Ellen and Diosa and me one person at a time and drove down to the ocean for Thai food.

"Do you think it's the end of the world?" said Peter.

"No," I said.

"You don't?"

"Every day I think it isn't and it's not," I said. "I've been right every time."

"And one day you could be wrong."

"It's been ending one person at a time for a long time," I said.

"This is a stupid topic," said Ellen. The season had just ended at the Theatricum and Ellen was adapting a novel about a woman who accidentally gets her egg mixed up with a bonobo sperm and has a halfling baby girl; the play is about the baby dealing with the world; intelligent, misunderstood innocence in a world of prejudice and hate.

"I wish I wrote that novel," I said.

"You did," said Diosa. "You gave it to some woman in Eugene named Andrea."

"That's the author's name," said Ellen.

"You write a lot," said Peter. "How do you keep writing when the times are so tumultuous?"

"It's a long story," I said.

Peter had turned sixty and started thinking about death. "It's too late," I told him, "you should have started a lot earlier." But that didn't stop Peter who was now reading Edgar Cayce and Shirley McClaine who were convincing him that we were all here with the problems of this life to work out the dilemmas we didn't solve in the last one, even people born poor and starving with no arms or legs.

"Too convenient," I said to him. "It means everybody gets what they deserve. Especially rich people."

"Maybe the world will end and none of us will have to come back," said Diosa.

"Exactly what we all deserve," said Ellen.

"We'll just come back on some other planet," said Peter.

"This is getting stupid again," said Ellen.

"I'm just trying to be open-minded," Peter said.

"You open your mind wide enough and somebody will put a foot in it," I said.

"Forgive him. He's autistic," said Diosa.

"That's convenient," said Peter. Then he made Diosa talk about eco-feminism in her work. "See," said Peter. "We're all trying to change the world for the better one person at a time. I'm teaching children how to solve their problems without drugs or violence. Ellen is writing about the inhumanity of humanity and the humanity of other species. Diosa is writing about how male values are destroying the planet."

"I'm writing a history of my pets," I said.

"I'm going to Prague," said Diosa.

"Frog?" I said.

"No," said Diosa. "Prague."

Fog?" I said.

"No," said Diosa. "Prague."

MASTERS OF THE
POETRY UNIVERSE

Time constantly goes from past to present and from present to future. This is true, but it is also true that time goes from future to present and from present to past.
Shunryu Suzuki

THAT'S RIGHT, PRAGUE. I should have known.

If you live in Los Angeles you can go to a poetry reading everyday. More than everyday. You can go to hundreds of poetry readings everyday. You think this is a movie industry town? A music industry town? A TV town? Entertainment industry? No. It's a poetry industry town. There are more poets than people here. More poets than cars. More poetry presses than designer dresses. Lots of people are only one person yet are several poets. My publisher at Disney, Randall Dodge, he's about eight different poets now, that way he's not publishing the same poet over and over. Actors are poets. Movie producers are poets. Administrative assistants, poets. The homeless are poets (they're often wine aficionados, too, but I don't even want to go there). Los Angeles is one long open mike poetry reading. You finish your poem, you jump in your car and drive to the next poetry reading and get in line. Is there an audience? No. Unless you count the other poets who are waiting to read. This is why, if you're a local, you have to get out of town, but poets from everywhere else flock here like, oh, well, like birds, like mating penguins, like, like, shit, I'm not a poet, like dolphins on a stick.

So we're on Melrose Avenue in Hollywood. Diosa just gave a reading at the Ruskin with David St. John and Ralph Angel, then they opened the mike and we slipped out under the tidal wave, like surfers ducking a break.

Outside the Chianti Cucina, who do we run into but Richard Katrovas and Mark Strand. I'd say they're famous poets, but if you're a normal person that wouldn't mean anything. Besides, they'd had to have just run into each other; Strand would never slum it with Katrovas. Diosa went way, way back with both those guys, long before me. In the poetry world, everybody goes way, way back. All poets have slept with each other either literally or metaphorically, you just have to assume that.

Katrovas, visiting from Kalamazoo, just came from UCLA where Greg Orr and Rita Dove, in from Charlottesville, just gave a reading. Strand didn't go because Orr wasn't famous enough and Dove was too famous and female to boot. He'd been at the Getty to hear Derek Walcott who he hated because he was so famous. Everybody was just catching their breath between afternoon and evening poetry readings.

"We're just grabbing a bite before heading out to hear Lady Gaga read at the Keystone Club," said Katrovas. "Or Carolyn Forche at the Viper Room."

"Maya Angelou is at the Hollywood Bowl," I said.

The two famous poets threw up.

"No one will be at the Keystone or Viper Room," said Diosa. "Viggo Mortenson is reading at Beyond Baroque."

"Holy shit!" Katrovas said.

"He keeps his horse at my new stable," I said. "The one he rode in that Arab horse race movie. Sometimes he gets riding and writing confused."

"I did for years," Diosa said. "And I don't even ride." She lit a cigarette and blew smoke at the poets.

"You don't get enough poetry in Kalamazoo?" I said to Katrovas.

"One reading a week," said Richard. "Here there's one a minute."

"How do you like living in New York?" Diosa said to Strand.

"This isn't New York?" Strand said.

"On television this is New York," I said. "In reality this is here."

"This is reality?" said Strand.

"You never mentioned he was funny," I said to Diosa.

"Wry," said Diosa.

Strand pulled a fountain pen from the inside pocket of his suit coat. "See this?" he said. "It's a time travel device. I'm going to use it to go back in time and destroy the internet."

"Somebody will just invent something worse," I said.

"No Facebook, no email, no e-publishing."

"A metaphor," said Diosa.

"You're going to handwrite the galaxy into oblivion," I said.

"No," said Strand, "literally. I'm going back with Kundera and Rushdie. We're going to save the poetry universe."

"You're taking fiction writers with you," I said.

"Geniuses," said Strand.

I figured there was only room in the world for one poetry genius.

"Triumvirates never work," I said. "Speaking of history."

"I'm hungry," said Katrovas. "Diosa, why don't you come to Prague with me for the summer? There are only a few poets there and I import all of them."

"Only if you invite Viggo," said Diosa.

"I think he and Duchovny are already doing St. Petersburg and Tanzania," said Katrovas.

Anyway, I guess that got Diosa thinking.

Meanwhile, back in the present, Strand took off.

"We better follow him," I said to Diosa. "I don't trust him with that fountain pen."

"He'll kill them both once he gets them back there," said Diosa.

"Back where?" I said.

"In time," Diosa said.

We followed Strand to a house on Mulholland overlooking the city, the lights of Los Angeles stretching out like a starry sky in southern Utah. It was Wally Shawn's place. Strand and Wally used to be skiing buddies back in Salt Lake City in the Eighties, then Wally moved here to write poetry. They met Kundera and Rushdie behind the house at the swimming pool. Nobody swims in their swimming pools in Los Angeles anymore, it's de classé, they all go to workout clubs where you aren't allowed to work out, only network (I got thrown out of the one I joined for breaking a sweat) but you have to have a pool to prove you can afford not to swim in it. There they were, sipping zinfandel and plotting to go back in time, destroy the internet, and murder the parents of all their contemporaries.

"We'll be the only ones left!" cackled Mark Strand. "We'll rule the World!"

"I never realized how much Mark Strand looked like Skeletor," whispered Diosa.

"Who remembers Skeletor?" I said.

"Who remembers Mark Strand?" Diosa said.

Well, soon they'd have to because he'd be the only writer left standing.

I don't like time travel or stories about it, so let's cut to the quick. They used Strand's fountain pen to create a wormhole, but Diosa and I slipped through it right on their heels, Wally Shawn yelling at our backs "Hey! Hey!" the way he always does. We found the three of them about to skewer Bill Gates' parents, got in a sword fight and killed all three. Wally Shawn was passed out on a lawn chair when we got back. Anyway, all three of them never existed, but nothing's changed. Nobody knew who they were before they never existed and nobody knows them now.

"Poor poets," said Diosa.

"Ah, poetry," I said. "Ah, humanity."

THE PRAGUE OF WAR

GEORGE HAD TAKEN APART our kitchen and we had to have coffee out. When we walked into the Mimosa Café, Julie, the barista, said, "Hey, where have you guys been?" Julie looked like you'd think a Julie would.

"I was just here yesterday," I said.

"But I wasn't here," said Julie. "I haven't seen Serum in weeks."

"He's just being Serum," Diosa said.

"He goes to the Water Lily now," I said, "so you'll wonder why he's not here and then he can dominate two places at once."

"Whoa," said Julie. "Totally mystical."

Really Serum was boycotting the Mimosa Café because its owner, Arlette, threw out all the pro-war types. "Where does she think she is, fucking Paris?" Serum said.

Now Diosa's cell went off. It was Serum.

"What are you doing in there?" said Serum. It was loud enough for anybody to hear. "Come to the Water Lily."

"How could he know?" said Julie.

"Because he's looking through the window?" I said.

"I thought he was at the Water Lily!" said Julie.

"Space travel," I said.

We went outside.

"I'm going to the Water Lily," Serum said. "Meet me."

"Want to come?" Diosa said to me.

"I can't talk to anyone yet, I'm not done with the Sports," I said. "I'm boycotting Serum's boycott."

"Come on," said Serum. "Indulge me."

Diosa grabbed both of my ears. "If I left you alone you wouldn't go anywhere or do anything. You'd ride your horse and run the dogs and lie on the floor with the cats."

I tried to think of something else I'd do, but she kind of had me. "Read books on the toilet?" I said.

So we got in the Ghost and drove down to Pine Tree Circle, the center of town, so to speak. Serum was driving his old, gray Nissan again because the BMW SUV that Robert Downey Jr. gave him broke down.

"You should see the fucking repair bill," Serum said. He was wearing all white linen that morning. His black, curly hair hit his shoulders.

"I told you," I said. "Free BMW's are like free dogs. Wait for the vet bill."

"It's a fucking BMW. It's never supposed to break fucking down," Serum said.

"My mother is channeling again," Diosa said.

"Does she know any mechanics?" Serum said.

"Wasn't Edgar Cayce a mechanic?" I said.

"It's how I spent my childhood," Diosa said. Because Jin-Jin couldn't write and channel at the same time, Diosa had to write it down for her. "Fifty volumes of iambic pentameter rhyme from the saints," Diosa said.

"God speaks in doggerel," I said.

"Does she believe in reincarnation?" said Serum.

"She believes in everything," Diosa said.

"It's why she's so at home in Malibu," I said.

"I just made my plans to visit her and now she's channeling again," Diosa said.

"How long?" said Serum.

"Two weeks."

"Two weeks, she's not fucking crazy, you are," said Serum.

"I'm channeling, too," I said. "It's how I'm writing my new book."

"But you're channeling to yourself," Diosa said.

"Doesn't everybody?" I said.

"He sends messages to himself," Diosa said to Serum. "From his own brain to his own brain."

Serum was laughing pretty hard. "Do you understand them?" he said.

"No," I said.

"Can we smoke a cigarette?" said Diosa.

We got up and sat outside the café at one of the small tables. Beyond the parking lot, the hills of Topanga rolled and spread, still green from the winter rain. Diosa gave Serum a cigarette and the two of them lit up.

"Look at us,' said Diosa.

"Beats fucking working," I said. Diosa lifted an unlit Parliament 100 to me but I turned it down. "Only before bed," I said, which I said every time. It became an awkward moment because Diosa usually met Serum here by herself. Smoked with him. Whatever else she did with him. And there were a thousand people, many of them celebrities, who would have given an arm, or at least a BMW, to be able to do that. Serum had a bevy of attractive, professional women who followed him around, even as he cooked dinner for his family, or cooked dinner for Diosa. They picked up after him, draped their doved hands upon his shoulders and back, asking him for advice on how to run their lives or how to crack an egg; he'd raise his arms, his robes falling from his wrists and say, "Leave me alone, run your own lives, crack your own eggs, go clean up or something," and they took it as if it fell from the lips of God.

They were wealthy people with great needs; they weren't at Temple, Mosque, Church or Zendo; they weren't following Suffi Imams or priests or paying psychotherapists; they could go anywhere in the world yet chose to drive (or have their chauffeurs drive them) up the winding trail to the top of Topanga, to the bottom of Serum's drive where they hiked a dirt path between boulders to his yurt for his expensive bad advice.

"Who you working with now?" asked Diosa.

"German super models," said Serum. "That chick on *House*. The head doctor. What's her name?"

If Serum was pretending that he couldn't remember her name then he was probably sleeping with her.

"Lisa Edelstein," said Diosa, who actually watched *House*.

"Cleavage," I said. "Tight skirts."

"You can meet her. I'll have a party at my place."

"When?"

"Tonight. Well, okay, two weeks."

By then, we'd fired George and Gendin had put our house back together.

When he beckoned, they came. And Diosa, Jesus and me went to Serum's for a dinner party. When it came to the sloppy Indian food, lamb or chicken in thick, curry gravy, Serum served up some good stuff. Serum kept chickens and goats and shot his own venison. He saw himself as a great cook. Mingo thought of himself as a great cook, too. They both saw themselves as great fathers and great cooks and when they first met over at my place they fought about child rearing and cooking. Other than that, it was great having great cooks around.

Three women, one of them Lisa Edelstein, bustled around in Serum's small kitchen following Serum. They all wore saris over tight, short-sleeve leotards, open, high heel sandals, toes painted by somebody else. Serum showed them some delicate, complicated way to break an egg without getting any shell in the pan. That's right, how to break an egg, after all. I walked into the kitchen with my wine, grabbed an egg, cracked it on the side of the bowl with one hand and dropped the egg into the bowl. The women were horrified.

"How are you assured there's no shell in there," said Lisa.

"I'm not," I said. "Who gives a fuck. It's a chicken egg not a chicken turd."

"It's unpleasant to discover a shell in your food," said Serum. "Don't you have an aesthetic?"

"You eat with your hands," I said.

"My right hand," said Serum. "That's the aesthetic."

"Because there's no toilet paper in Asia," I said.

"It's about meditation, concentration," Lisa Edelstein said to me.

"I'm pretty concentrated," I said.

There was a tall guy, gray blond hair down to his shoulders, glasses, standing in the corner, watching. He was a director. The writers are short, bald, and wear baseball hats. There were several of those scurrying around outside.

"Sounds like you two go back a long ways," the director said.

"NoCal in 1979," I said to him.

"We ran into each other in Red Rock," said Serum.

"Old friends reunited, a great story," the director said.

"We're not friends," I said.

We all stared at each other for a moment. Then Serum guffawed. That was good enough for me and I went outside to sit next to Diosa by the fire.

"How did it go?" said Diosa.

"We're invited to a movie screening. I improperly smashed an egg," I said.

"The collateral damage was horrific. Everybody's concentration was destroyed."

"I'd better get in there," said Diosa.

Jesus was over by the hot tub with Ashley and Celine, Serum's kids, signing autographs. Peacocks wandered amidst the guests. I stood up and a burly guy grabbed me from behind, turned me around and kissed me on the lips.

"Stacy!" he said.

"Stacy?"

"Stacy Keach. We're old friends!"

"How good of friends are you with Stacy Keach if you're kissing me?"

"You're not Stacy Keach?" said the burly guy. "Are you Donald Sutherland?"

"You're confusing Stacy Keach with Donald Sutherland?" I said. Besides I'm way younger, thinner, and better looking than either of those guys.

He tried to say Jeff but I stopped him. "Don't say Jeff Bridges," I said.

"Nick Nolte," said the Burly guy.

"Shark," I said. "Shark Rosenthal."

"I never heard of him," he said.

Then Sting showed up with Robert Downey Jr., but lucky for them nobody recognized them.

Diosa emerged from the house, cigarette and wine glass. "I've decided," she said. "I'm going to Prague."

"That's great," I said to her, "when do we leave?"

"I didn't say we were going to Prague, I said I was going to Prague," Diosa said.

"By yourself?"

"I need to be alone."

"You won't be alone in Prague," I said. "It's full of people and lascivious American poets."

"It's what I want to do, Shark," said Diosa. "I can do what I want."

"Okay," I said. "I'm going to Hawaii."

"You can't go to Hawaii without me," said Diosa. "Hawaii is a vacation."

"I'll go to a Zendo. I'll concentrate a lot."

"If you go to Hawaii I'm leaving you," said Diosa.

"You're leaving me to go to Prague," I said.

"I'll leave you when I get back."

Anyway, Diosa went to Prague. I tried to go to Hawaii but ended up in Uruguay instead. The ticket agent was Argentinean and they pronounce Uruguay "Hawaii." Go figure. The surfing is lousy in Montevideo.

Meanwhile, back in Prague, Diosa was having a lousy time. We ran up a twenty thousand dollar international cell phone bill. I had to refinance the house.

"Everybody speaks Czech here," said Diosa. "The rest are poets."

There's a fine line between heaven and hell.

She emailed me:

Mi Tiburon:
el mar es muy gentil aqui,
verde, y suave. El cielo es
gris, como tus gatos favoritos.
El sol es muy fuerte.
La luna no esta llena.

je pense a ti.

Diosa

Who cares if she wasn't on the ocean and she mixed Spanish and French. She was a surrealist.

I wrote her back.

Mi amor:
aqui la luna no esta llena
ni media llena
pero media vacua
como mi corozon

traje su luz pronto

Su Tiburon

"Venga, mi amor," said Diosa. "Bring Jesus. Come to Prague."

Hell, it was cheaper than the phone.

JESUS IS TRANSFIGURED

PRAGUE WAS RAINY AND COLD. Summer and cold. A day of cold
drizzle, then the next day broke with sun until the thunderheads gathered in
the afternoon, roaring and dumping sheets of rain.

At mid-day Diosa and me and Jesus took the subway from Mala Strana
to the Mustek station at the bottom of Wenceslas Square. We walked toward
the National Museum, hung a right on Vadichova, and went in the Lanhaum
Gallerie to look at an exhibition of photography by Arabs. Czechs, especially
Pragues, love photography. The Arab men took pictures of themselves, of
sheiks, of kings, tribal leaders, military officers. The women took pictures of
poor women, working women, women with children, women buried under
burkhas and robes; a woman against a wall of Arabic, she, shrouded in sheets
covered with Arabic script that blended into the wall. Women were not
permitted to write in Arabic script.

"Well," said Jesus, "guess that says it."

Guess it did.

We ate on the square, in one of those labyrinthine restaurants that
descended and descended in arcs and twists, its ancient walls lit with
fluorescent light, the music, lousy Czech pop imitating lousy American pop,
the vocalist not even understanding his own words. We ate duck sausage,
garlic soup; Czech stuff. The beer, Krusevice, was excellent. Jesus and Diosa

had desert, strawberries in thick, sweet cream. I drank grappa. It's Prague, you wait interminably for the bill.

Suddenly, a crowd of people began flowing into the restaurant, excited and wet. Thunder rumbled through the stairwells and hallways. Me and Diosa and Jesus made our way to the front of the restaurant where people crowded in the foyer. Outside, rain came down like bombs, pounding the cobblestone, wrecking umbrellas, drowning sound. On the street, people huddled in doorways and under ledges as the streets began to flood. And inside, a buzz of wonderment. Lightning flashed. Seconds later, a crack of thunder.

"It's close," said Diosa.

"Yes," I said.

"Bathroom," Diosa said, and meandered through the crowded vestibule, leaving Jesus and me at the edge of the radical downpour.

Then Jesus did the most unusual thing. She stepped out, into the driving rain. She turned back to me. Thunder and lightning crackled simultaneously. The world went white. On either side of Jesus stood two figures, like her, shining. On her left, Marlalyn Monroe. On her right, Karl Marx. Then the halo of light faded. The rain let up and Jesus came back into the restaurant.

"Don't tell anyone about this, Father," Jesus said.

FOR JIMMY SKAGGS

I'VE GOT A WHOLE BOOK about Prague, but this book isn't about Prague, though I suppose I could set the Prague book here, at Universal Studios. No, this book is about Los Angeles and here in Los Angeles I always celebrate three Thanksgivings: Canadian Thanksgiving on the second weekend of October, regular American Thanksgiving, and Lesbian thanksgiving on Gertrude Stein's birthday in February. I've done it for decades.

That Thanksgiving, before we went to Prague, the actor Jimmy Skaggs came with his wife, actress and director, Virginia Morris. We all went back to the early Eighties when Diosa was workshopping plays at Sundance. I met Robert Redford. He was very handsome but only four foot three. Virginia and Jimmy were both artists, but Jimmy made a fortune when he learned to hit the mark and say "I'm going to blow your fucking head off!" He was the last bad guy to die in a lot of big *Lethal Weapon* type movies. You've seen him a hundred times, even if you didn't know it. You've probably seen the unknown people like Jimmy more than you've seen the famous ones.

Having heard the day before that he had lung cancer, Jimmy sat there the whole night and said nothing about it, though he was oddly quiet. Anyway, he told me and Diosa in February during brunch at the Cheesecake Factory in Pasadena. He'd just finished a run of chemo.

"I didn't want to ruin Thanksgiving," Jimmy said. "Anyway, the doctor says I'm clean. They got it. My chemo tech says nobody with lung cancer ever lives."

After brunch we went to a close-out party at Book Alley, the used bookstore owned by Peter Hay, a retired dramaturg who'd been at Sundance with us. Peter had published a biography of Hannah Senesh. They made a movie of it. He made a little money and was heading to Vancouver to retire. After we got there Jimmy sat off to the side, by himself. I went over and sat next to him; folding chairs, three walls of books.

"I'm not going to die, Shark," Jimmy said.

"It's okay to die," I said. "It's okay. We're going to die."

"It's not okay. I'm not going to," Jimmy said.

Jimmy died in July when we were in Prague.

And that next November, for the first time in memory, in honor of Jimmy I didn't cook Thanksgiving. But that night they played *The Pirate Movie* on Starz and there he was.

ARE WE NOT THERE YET?
OR
DAZE OF FUTURE PAST

ARI CAUGHT ME in my office.

"How'd you know I was here?" I said.

"I know everything, but it's over. I've been let go."

"Impossible," I said.

"J.K. Weakhart, head of Rhetoric and Comp," said Ari.

"Professional jealousy," I said. "Kids were becoming literate. The improvements were too obvious."

"I guess that was a slip up. He planted a student at a bar and I drank a beer with her. No contact with students off campus."

"I travel with students," I said.

"That's a class."

"Phil Filson has got three pregnant."

"That's in his office," said Ari.

"You going back to Hollywood?" I said.

"I guess. The Academy is just too cutthroat." He went to my computer, turned it on and got on some kind of site, like a secret Jesuit Facebook. "Look at all this encrypted back and forth between the Dean, the VP, the Provost, and the President. Your D'Asheena thing is coming to a head."

"I better hide," I said.

"Good luck," said Ari and disappeared into the glare of the sun bouncing off the Pacific. He's out there somewhere now, behind the scenes, making Armenian babies.

"What a world! What a world!" I said. I shut down my computer and pulled my phone out of the wall. Shut off my cell phone. But it was too late. An envelope was slipped under my door.

"I'm ignoring that!" I shouted.

"If you don't open it, it will explode in thirty seconds," said a small voice.

I opened it. I'd been summoned to the Office of the President of the University of La-La Holy.

Somehow the President's office seemed bigger than the building that enclosed it, cavernous, office furniture made for giants, a wooden tribunal two stories high on top of which sat three hooded figures. It was like one of those trials on *Star Trek*.

"I'm innocent," I said.

"This has nothin' to do with guilt or innocence," said the figure in the center. "We're sending you to India. Study abroad." I noticed now that they were smoking cigars and drinking something that looked like cognac.

"I don't want to go to India."

"You'll love it."

"The last two guys you sent to India died," I said.

"They were old and refusing to retire," said the hooded judge.

"I don't want to retire," I said. "I want to live! Live!"

"While you're there, D'Asheena gets all A's. We graduate her on out of here, get her a job in African-American Studies at Fordham.

"Fordham," I said. "Jesuit."

"That's right. We took care of your little girlfriend, too."

"What little girlfriend?"

"Riordon. Caught her drinking off campus with her T.A."

"Kardashian?"

"Two birds with one stone," said the hooded judge. "We pulled her scholarship. Gave her a free ride to Gonzaga."

The northernmost Jesuit outpost.

"We bought Mervyn Delamore a Gay Studies Chair at Humboldt State. There'll be nobody left. It's flushed."

"Hynde," I said.

"Hynde is our stooge. Besides, he opens his trap he'll be teaching Braille in Haiti. You go to India, come back in a year under an assumed name. That's that. Nobody remembers nothin'.

"Egg," I said.

"Will be President at USF."

"The *La-La Holyan*," I said.

"Right. They don't remember what they wrote yesterday."

"Why not get rid of me?"

"We're gettin' rid of you. Besides, you work cheap. We fire you we got to replace you with an ethnic type. They're expensive. But when you get back, no more talking in the classroom for you. No more imparting information. Break them into small groups. Let them talk to each other. You give two grades, Pass A, Fail B."

"In India?"

"Your whole roster's fake. Get there and lie low."

"Can I take Diosa and Jesus?"

"You think we want Jesus on this campus?" said the president.

"You'll love India," I said to Jesus that night. "There's lots of other Gods there. You'll have a social life."

"And we'll need shoes!" said Diosa, ever the satirist of her own life. "In India you need lots and lots of shoes. Shoes for India!"

Mingo and Gabriela came over and we partied like it was 1999. On D-Day they drove us to the airport. We were off, off, off! But that's another story, for another time, in a galaxy far, far away.

PREFACE
WHAT IS MAGIC JOURNALISM?

A MAGIC JOURNALIST understands that the narrative essay becomes a living metaphor of an inexpressible truth.

When I was living in the Himalayas I wrote almost everyday and some of this writing became the seeds of my first book of Magic Journalism, *Are We Not There Yet? Travels in Nepal, North India, and Bhutan.* In India the Hindus and the Buddhists, too, believe in the concept of *maya*, that is, that the world is illusory, and I began to write about that and about how that concept permeated Indian life. I wanted to write about how the concept of maya unconsciously operated in America and came to the discovery that there were many illusions Americans believed, from life-time warranties to police protection to believing that the thing you bought and paid for will be delivered to your house, or believing you lived in a functioning home or cosmos.

Yet it wasn't so much watching and thinking and reporting that led me to the fundamental difference between American and Indian maya, but the act of writing about it. Reading what I wrote made me realize that in India reality is illusion and in America illusion is reality. When a traditional journalist writes about something, she starts out and ends with the thing she's writing about. The Magic Journalist doesn't know what he's writing about until after he's written it. In fact, I barely knew what this book was about until I'd re-read it fifty times and re-written it ten more. What does it mean? Would you believe me if I said I didn't know?

Magic Journalism doesn't happen in front of you, it happens behind you. It's informed by ideas that are impossible to believe and overdetermined by the conviction that those are the best kind. It's not about mystery or recording mystery. In fact, I'm fed up with mystery, however fond I am of enigma, which unlike mystery can be unraveled into beauty and, as Emily Dickinson suggests, placed next to truth in a grave. No, Emily Dickinson was not a Magic Journalist.

Magic Journalism comprehends the tenuous relationship between events and the act of writing about them, and the even more tenuous event of reading it. In a Magic Journalist essay reality creeps up on you until it tips over into the magical, the absurd, the lyrical, the really real. It's not about a given event, but an essential event, no matter how many actual events are involved. If a journalist investigates the facts, the New Journalist the issues, the Gonzo journalist the self, the creative non-fiction writer the personal experience, the Magic Journalist investigates the metaphor of living.

Because of their dependence on reporting, the previous incarnations of journalism have been adamantly naïve in regard to the relationship of language to the world. There's a world out there and there are true things in it. These things are facts. They are events that happened. The traditional journalist, using words, tries to find these facts and report them. Though we can find root and reason to take us all the way back to Xenophon and Herodotus, and in the States, at least Thoreau, the New Journalism, which arose in the Sixties (Truman Capote, Norman Mailer, John McPhee, Joan Didion, Susan Sontag), was the first journalism, as such, to self consciously employ fiction techniques: narration, scene setting, scene and dialogue, to tell the story of an investigation, though the aim was still that of Ernest Hemingway's non-fiction, you had to make choices about what you were going to depict in order to get to the true story. But the New Journalist is still after the facts; the thrust is still objective.

Closely on its heels came the Gonzo Journalism of Hunter S. Thompson (should I add Kathy Acker?) where the only attainable truths are seen through a subjective, if not radically distorted, lens. When Gonzo Journalism reaches hyperbole it comes closest to Magic Journalism, but it still engenders a naïve commitment to recording facts, no matter how subjective, and often implies that subjective experience is a means for getting at the truth. The progenitors of Gonzo Journalism were Beats, Jack Kerouac in *Satori in Paris* in particular, eliding into William Burroughs' *Junky*, with tentacles reaching into autobiographical narrative, particularly the "naked" writing of the Seventies like Kate Millet's *Flying* and Rita Mae Brown's *Ruby Fruit Jungle*. American journalism, like its literature, has its Romantic (subjective truth) and Realist (objective truth) wings.

Magic Journalism is the first self-consciously post-modern journalism. I mean that it's the first journalism that realizes that facts, either objective or subjective, do not lie behind words. In fact, that double entendre (to lie) is kind of what it's all about. The Magic Journalist realizes that as soon as she writes about something it becomes very different than what might have happened.

How did a sculpture garden made up of used furniture and broken machines get in my front yard? It grew out of the things that never got into my house. Things I ordered by catalogue or telephone or the internet and never really arrived, or arrived in pieces that no one, no person or robot or computer or machine had ever bothered to put together. They're just like the things inside my house that appear to have been put together, but really have just fallen into entity status by chance. Nothing in our lives really works. Nothing connects from one moment to the next but our belief that things are working. There is no difference between the life inside my home and the sculpture garden on my lawn, or the broken bus down the road that those meth addicts are living in. My friend Stephanie isn't homeless, she's living in a one room camper with one extension cord and no running water. There are homeless folks living under my sculpture garden right now! Call CNN! Wait till I tell the *LA Times*!

But a regular journalist, be he print or broadcasting, or blogging on the internet, likely wouldn't touch this. Because it's so true it's happening everywhere, on the Pacific Palisades and Venice Beach, in Hollywood, Oakwood, South LA, Compton, Chatsworth, New York City, Philadelphia, everywhere. Where do you live?

If a journalist did take a look at my front yard, she'd have to make it special. She might try to investigate why and how it happened, assuming that there would be some facts back there that led to the truth. A Magic Journalist knows there aren't any. A Gonzo Journalist would have gotten stoned and written about that. A creative non-fiction writer would only write about this if it happened to him, maybe crawl under some of my junk for a week and commune with my tenants. He'd make it personal, using fiction techniques to write about it, then trying at the end of the narrative to leap to a statement about how it reflects upon our society. A Magic Journalist understands that the narrative essay becomes a living metaphor of an inexpressible truth.

Magic Journalism denies the subjective-objective dualism, the word-fact dualism, it finds the idea of a *true story* to be absurd, not that we shouldn't try to tell them. The difference between previous journalistic forms and Magic Journalism is like the difference between pottery and ceramic sculpture, between photography and painting, between Newtonian physics and Einstein's relativity, between facts and processes. Magic Journalism doesn't report, it doesn't re-create, it creates. The guiding hand is aesthetic not practical. This isn't to deny the value of pottery, photography, reporting, re-creating, and Newton. Of course anybody who's been around the deconstruction block a few times could argue that these distinctions I've just made are spurious. Well, welcome to post-modernity. For my part, as a Magic Journalist, I make them whether spurious or not.

So you might now think that Magic Journalism is just a misnomer; that really I'm just talking about writing fiction. Allow me to say that if you get caught up on things like truth and facts (in my fiction classes we like to call them ficts), or whether or not something was made up, you'll never figure out the difference between fiction and non-fiction at all. Part of the difference is just a matter of conviction (and just because that rhymes, it doesn't make it poetry). Speaking of conviction, in this country you could go to jail for writing non-fiction, but not for fiction, though in other countries your fiction could get you killed. More to the point, the difference between the two has more to do with the structure and composition of the completed text, the way the issues of the narrative emerge, the ways in which the narrative flirts with genre or genres (literary and non-literary), the ways chronology and causality are implied from beginning to end. Is Maxine Hong Kingston's *The Woman Warrior* memoir or fiction? You tell me. Okay, I'll tell you. It's proto-Magic Journalism.

Words are the miraculous scalpel with which miracles are dissected. Magic Journalism doesn't write about miracles because the world is already miraculous enough, but look, here, for the miracle, and there, behind you, the magic is at work, not like magic tricks, but really real magic, and reality, whether in India or Los Angeles, will tip over into it if you're willing to wait for what's behind you to jump on your back. So you have to go hunting and you have to wrestle, whether you're doing it in a Himalayan rain forest, in an alley in Kathmandu, on a bus in LA or in a shack in Topanga Canyon a hundred feet above an overlook called "Heaven."

A Magic Journalist understands that the narrative essay becomes a living metaphor of an inexpressible truth.

So go to that haunted house, go on a ghost hunt. You won't find any ghosts. But if you think your essay will be about finding ghosts or not finding them, if you think it's about what happened to you, then you're all wet, because the metaphor of the ghost hunt has already transcended any facts about ghosts or your personal experience in looking for them. Find that metaphor. I live my life inside myself with a ghost I barely know. That's Magic Journalism.

CHUCK ROSENTHAL is the author of seven published novels: the Loop Trilogy—*Loop's Progress, Experiments With Life and Deaf,* and *Loop's End—Elena of the Stars; Avatar Angel, the Last Novel of Jack Kerouac; My Mistress, Humanity;* and *The Heart of Mars.* He's the author of a memoir, *Never Let Me Go,* and a book of Magic Journalism, *Are We Not There Yet? Travels in Nepal, North India, and Bhutan.* He has just completed another novel, *Annie and Bird,* and is working on a book about animal cognition entitled *Pet Me While I Eat.* He lives in Topanga Canyon with poet Gail Wronsky (Diosa). Jesus changed her name to Marlena Dali and moved to Sydney, Australia.

MORE PRAISE FOR *WEST OF EDEN*

Chuck Rosenthal's *West of Eden* will demand that even the most skeptical and shrewd of readers should prepare for a fresh abundance of hilarity and the absurd, woven delicately with segments of beauty, sadness, and irony. One cannot argue that Rosenthal, nor this body of work, stands amidst or against the literary tradition of Southern California because *West of Eden* is unlike anything written. To understand this Magical Journalism, one need not be an adroit ledger and preacher of non-fiction, fiction, or even literary post-structuralism. The book resists rigid definitions, just as we readers should forever seek what is fresh and new outside of our habitual and stifling confines. To read these narrative bits and pieces and to indulge their relentlessly funny, hapless, poetic, and truth-seeking narrator is to engage the ghosts—both attendant and not—within us all.

—Cody Todd, author of *To Frankenstein, My Father* (Proem Press) and the Co-Creator of The Offending Adam.

TITLES FROM

WHAT BOOKS PRESS

POETRY

Molly Bendall & Gail Wronsky, *Bling & Fringe (The L.A. Poems)*

Kevin Cantwell, *One of Those Russian Novels*

Ramón García, *Other Countries*

Karen Kevorkian, *Lizard Dream*

Gail Wronsky, *So Quick Bright Things*
BILINGUAL, SPANISH TRANSLATED BY ALICIA PARTNOY

FICTION

François Camoin, *April, May, and So On*

A.W. DeAnnuntis, *Master Siger's Dream*

A.W. DeAnnuntis, *The Mermaid at the Americana Arms Motel*

Katharine Haake, *The Origin of Stars and Other Stories*

Katharine Haake, *The Time of Quarantine*

Mona Houghton, *Frottage & Even As We Speak: Two Novellas*

Chuck Rosenthal, *Coyote O'Donohughe's History of Texas*

MAGIC JOURNALISM

Chuck Rosenthal, *Are We Not There Yet? Travels in Nepal, North India, and Bhutan*

Chuck Rosenthal, *West of Eden: A Life in 21st Century Los Angeles*

ART

Gronk, *A Giant Claw*
BILINGUAL, SPANISH

WHAT
BOOKS
PRESS

LOS ANGELES

What Books Press books may be ordered from:
SPDBOOKS.ORG | ORDERS@SPDBOOKS.ORG | (800) 869 7553 | AMAZON.COM

Visit our website at
WHATBOOKSPRESS.COM